Parenting Traumatized Children with Developmental Differences

of related interest

An Introduction to Autism Spectrum Disorder
for Adoptive and Foster Families
How to Understand and Help Your Child
Katie Hunt and Helen Rodwell
ISBN 978 1 78592 405 7
eISBN 978 1 78450 759 6

Why Can't My Child Behave?
Empathic Parenting Strategies that Work for Adoptive and Foster Families
Dr Amber Elliott
ISBN 978 1 84905 339 6
eISBN 978 0 85700 671 4

Parenting Strategies to Help Adopted and
Fostered Children with Their Behaviour
Trauma-Informed Guidance and Action Charts
Christine Gordon
Illustrated by Corinne Watt
ISBN 978 1 78592 386 9
eISBN 978 1 78450 738 1

The Secrets of Successful Adoptive Parenting
Practical Advice and Strategies to Help with
Emotional and Behavioural Challenges
Sophie Ashton
Foreword by Bryan Post
ISBN 978 1 78592 078 3
eISBN 978 1 78450 340 6

The A–Z of Therapeutic Parenting
Strategies and Solutions
Sarah Naish
ISBN 978 1 78592 376 0
eISBN 978 1 78450 732 9
Part of the Therapeutic Parenting Books *series*

The Simple Guide to Child Trauma
What It Is and How to Help
Betsy de Thierry
Foreword by David Shemmings
Illustrated by Emma Reeves
ISBN 978 1 78592 136 0
eISBN 978 1 78450 401 4
Part of the Simple Guides *series*

PARENTING TRAUMATIZED CHILDREN WITH DEVELOPMENTAL DIFFERENCES

Strategies to Help Your Child's Sensory Processing, Language Development, Executive Function and Challenging Behaviours

Dr Sara McLean

Jessica Kingsley *Publishers*
London and Philadelphia

First published in 2019
by Jessica Kingsley Publishers
73 Collier Street
London N1 9BE, UK
and
400 Market Street, Suite 400
Philadelphia, PA 19106, USA

www.jkp.com

Copyright © Dr Sara McLean 2019

Library of Congress Cataloging in Publication Data
A CIP catalog record for this book is available from the Library of Congress

British Library Cataloguing in Publication Data
A CIP catalogue record for this book is available from the British Library

ISBN 978 1 78592 433 0
eISBN 978 1 78450 805 0

Printed and bound in the United States

Contents

Acknowledgements

The author is grateful to the Eureka Benevolent Foundation for its support in developing resources for foster parents, and for permission to adapt portions of this work. The author would also like to thank the many foster parents who have supported her work.

This book provides general educational information only, and is not intended as a substitute for professional assessment and intervention.

Introduction

Why read this book?

If you are a foster carer or adoptive parent who is struggling to support a child with significant behavioural issues, then this book is relevant to you.

As any foster or adoptive parent knows, behavioural problems are common amongst foster and adopted children, and this book is written with both carers' and children's needs in mind.

Have you have noticed any of the following?

- You find that the parenting approaches you have used before aren't working.

- Your child has difficulty following instructions.

- Your child has difficulty in seeing things through.

- Your child has difficulty in getting started on tasks.

- Your child seems deliberately non-compliant.

- Your child has trouble managing their behaviour.

- Your child seems to explode without apparent reason.

- You find yourself wondering why your child is more difficult to support than other children.

- You are starting to doubt your own abilities as a foster or adoptive parent.

If any of the above are true for you, then it could be worth working through the chapters in this book. This book introduces the concept of *developmental differences* amongst children in out of home care and explains what a child's developmental differences might mean for their behaviour.

What are developmental differences?

Our understanding of the relationship between early childhood adversity and brain development is rapidly developing (see Box 2, Chapter 1). This emerging knowledge is helping us to better understand how the brain development of children who have experienced adversity differs from other children because of their very different developmental experiences.

This book introduces the concept of developmental difference as a hallmark characteristic of many children who come into foster or adoptive care. Developmental difference is a term that I have introduced to describe key characteristics of children who have experienced early adversity: 'developmental' because these issues arise in the context of their early development; and 'difference' because the term reflects patterns of vulnerability and difference when compared with other children. Children placed in foster or adoptive care are likely to experience one or more interrelated areas of developmental difference and these are the focus of this book.

In this book, I describe what these developmental differences mean for caregiving, discipline and behaviour, and I provide concrete tips on how to support children with any of these developmental differences.

The impact of early adversity on brain development is a rapidly developing area of research. This is not a book full of research information, although I've included references for you to follow up if you are interested. The purpose of this book is to provide you with practical strategies to support children who are living with one or more areas of developmental difference.

My approach to supporting children focuses on the functional and trans-diagnostic difficulties that children experience. Trans-diagnostic difficulties refer to the kind of skills that children who have been given a range of diagnostic labels struggle with (e.g. ADHD, oppositional defiant disorder, conduct disorder.) This means that I encourage parents to 'look beyond' the child's current diagnosis and instead to focus on strengthening the areas of developmental difference that are needed to support their child right now. As we'll see, children with a range of developmental differences need to be supported in similar ways.

First, we need to adjust our expectations for a child. We need to understand 'What's different for this child?' rather than 'What's wrong with this child?' Second, we need to modify the child's environment, making it easier for the child to experience success. Finally, we need to teach the child the skills and competencies that they may be missing. We'll talk more about what all this means throughout this book.

- In Chapter 1 we'll look at the types of adversity that children can face. We'll look at how these experiences contribute to areas of developmental difference. I've also included some of the readily available literature on brain development and early adversity for those of you who are interested in reading further.

- Chapter 2 will provide a guide to the key developmental milestones at each developmental stage, and provide indicators of developmental delay for each developmental stage.

- In Chapter 3 we'll look at the main reasons that children can have challenging behaviour. We'll identify the clues that behaviour is driven by developmental difference as opposed to other possible causes. This chapter will also outline some principles for approaching behavioural concerns in children.

- In Chapter 4 we will introduce the first of the developmental differences – sensory regulation difficulties (managing how our body reacts to the sensory world) – and describe how to identify and support children with these sensory processing issues.

- Chapter 5 will introduce developmental differences in language and communication and describe how to identify and support children with language and communication difficulties.

- In Chapter 6 we will look at how to identify and support children with developmental difference in the capacity for emotional regulation (managing how our body reacts to strong emotions). We'll look at strategies for building children's emotional literacy.

- Chapter 7 will introduce the concept of executive functioning (the way the brain organizes thinking and memory) and memory difficulty (and what this developmental difference means for children's flexible thinking, planning and organization skills). We'll look at the strategies to support the development of executive functioning and memory skills in children with this developmental difference.

- Chapter 8 will introduce the emerging evidence on children's social processing bias (the way we interpret social situations and information), and what this means for children with this developmental difference.

- In Chapter 9 we'll look at how to communicate information about your child's developmental differences to key professionals in your child's life (such as their caseworker and their teacher).

- In Chapter 10, we'll re-visit and summarize the key principles for supporting your child.

- Appendices 1–3 contain blank sensory sheets that you can copy and tailor to your child. They can be reprinted and updated when your strategies are adapted as your child grows older.

This book is designed to *augment* what you are probably doing already to support your child. The foundation of high quality caregiving is safe and nurturing parenting together with age-appropriate boundaries and consequences. The strategies in this book are not intended as a *substitute* for high quality parenting; high quality nurturing care is *necessary* but may not be *sufficient* to meet the needs of children with developmental difference.

This book provides a toolkit of options and ideas in the case where extra support might be needed and where traditional discipline has not been effective. I hope it provides you with strategies for supporting your child right now, with enough information to determine when further support might be needed and also with the information you need to advocate on your child's behalf.

Chapter 1

Early Adversity and Developmental Difference

We'll begin by exploring what we know about the impact of early life adversity on children's development. There are two main areas of children's development that are affected by adverse caregiving experiences.

First, early adversity affects children's cognitive development (the development of children's thinking, memory and problem-solving skills) in a range of areas. We now believe that early adversity affects brain development in the areas that underpin children's social, cognitive and behavioural functioning. These are the developmental differences we'll discuss in the remaining chapters of this book.

The second area of children's development that is affected by early adversity is the child's understanding of themselves, of adults and of relationships. We typically refer to this as a child's 'attachment experience'. There are many books that discuss the relationship between early adversity and a child's attachment relationship, so this won't be a primary focus of this book, but I will briefly explain what it means.

What does a child's 'attachment experience' mean? As a result of a child's early caregiving experience, they form a belief about how reliable and trustworthy adults are and how they need to behave towards adults in order to elicit caregiving and attention. Although this book does not deal with a child's attachment in detail we'll touch on this topic briefly now and re-visit this in Chapter 3, when we discuss the main reasons for challenging behaviour, and I will also give recommendations for further reading for those readers who do want to dig deeper.

Let's look briefly at the impact of early adversity on children's attachment relationships, before moving on to look at developmental differences in more detail.

Early adversity and the attachment relationship

It is likely that at some level your child's early caregiving experiences have left them with a view of adults as unsafe, unresponsive or unreliable. As the significant adult in your child's life, you are able to offer them an alternative experience of adults: as being safe and reliable and of being capable of providing nurturing and responsive care. No matter how loving, safe and nurturing you may be as a foster carer or adoptive parent, however, your child *does not always see you this way*. It is important to understand what your child's implicit beliefs about relationships might be as this will affect how your child reacts to you, particularly in times of stress.

If you are raising a foster or adopted child, you can guess that the significant adults in your child's early life may have disciplined them in harsh or inconsistent ways. Many of the parents referred to child protection services are struggling with issues that seriously affect their capacity and ability to parent with the structure, routine and predictability needed at each developmental stage. Abusive or neglectful families are commonly dealing with:

- *Alcohol and drug abuse issues*, meaning that children can be exposed to inconsistent parenting, supervisory and physical neglect, and lack of predictable routines.

- *Unmanaged mental health issues* such as ongoing depression and psychosis (suffering from hallucinations and delusional beliefs), often leading to child neglect; exposure to irrational parental beliefs; restricted social interactions and being compelled to take on the parental role in the family.

- *Family and intimate partner violence,* meaning that children are exposed to high levels of fear and trauma; may have witnessed violence against a parent; and can be compelled to take on a parental role in the family or compelled to identify with the violent parent.

- *Parents re-living their own trauma histories,* meaning that parents can be triggered to remember their own traumatic events by everyday parenting activities. This often means that parents are psychologically unavailable or distant to their children.

All of these issues, and others, can mean that parents are absorbed in their own thoughts, feelings and activities. They do not have the energy or time needed to provide the structure, consistency and follow through necessary for children's development.

These experiences affect how safe a child feels; how safe they feel other people are; and how much they feel that others can be relied on to do what they promise. As a result, children form an unspoken belief about how they should behave around adults who are important to them; and about what they need to do to elicit adults' attention and affection.

Children's early experience of relationships shapes their idea of what it means to be cared for by an adult. It shapes their belief about their role in a family and about how conflicts are resolved in families. As a result of their early experiences of being in a family, children form implicit (unconscious) beliefs about themselves and others. This is really what people mean when they talk about a child's attachment history. It's their unspoken beliefs about themselves, about adults and about how to be in the world (see McLean, 2016a for more detailed information about attachment amongst children in care).

Some children are raised with extremely inconsistent parenting, in which their primary caregiver is both frightening and dangerous, and simultaneously needy and dependent on them. These children appear more likely to develop chaotic and disorganized beliefs about relationships and may be more likely to engage in compulsive behaviour as they get older.

Some children learn that the safest thing to do is to always anticipate and pre-empt danger. These children learn to stay safe by compulsively controlling others.

Other children learn to keep themselves safe by always taking care of others (compulsive caretaking). These children have learned to engage in compulsive behaviours (controlling or caretaking) because they feel it keeps them safe in an otherwise inconsistent and frightening world.

Other children form a more consistent set of beliefs about being cared for. Here I've outlined some of these unspoken beliefs about adults and what these might mean for children's behaviour:

Your child's caregiving	Your child's unspoken beliefs	Your child's behaviour towards you
Your child experienced relatively consistent caregiving, in which they felt that their caregivers were emotionally 'available' but in a conditional way: provided that your child was not too emotionally demanding	If I express emotions or needs, adults will get angry or reject me I can ensure my caregiver stays close if I just keep my feelings to myself If I risk being close, I risk rejection	This may mean your child is uncomfortable with freely expressing emotions and may instead express feelings as challenging behaviour Your child may have learned to use behaviour to keep you at their preferred emotional distance (not to let you get too close) Your child could have a restricted range of emotions, appear self-reliant and emotionally over-controlled
Your child experienced relatively consistent caregiving, in which they felt that their caregivers were emotionally 'available' but in a conditional way: provided that your child exaggerated their needs and their dependence	If I am overly dramatic and needy, I can get adults' attention I need to keep my caregiver close at hand I need to really exaggerate my needs in order to be noticed If I cope, I will be abandoned	This may mean your child is uncomfortable with being self-reliant and independent Your child may have learned to use attention-seeking and dependent behaviour to keep you close at hand Your child may be overly dramatic, dependent and emotionally under-regulated

cont.

Your child experienced inconsistent and frightening caregiving	I am helpless I am unable to get my needs met Adults are scary Adults need looking after	Your child may engage in compulsive controlling/ parenting behaviour, dismissing the needs of others Your child may engage in compulsively caretaking, neglecting their own needs

Once children are placed into a foster or adoptive home we expect that they will feel safe and begin to thrive. It can be disheartening when this doesn't happen quickly. It can be useful to ask yourself about what your child's early caregiving experiences might have 'taught' them about themselves and about the significant adults in their life. These unspoken 'attachment' beliefs are often behind behaviour that's related to feelings of intimacy and vulnerability – it keeps adults within their comfort zone (we'll return to this in Chapter 3 when we discuss 'boundary behaviour').

BOX 1
What is cognitive development?

Cognitive development refers to the process of acquiring increasingly advanced reasoning and problem-solving ability, from infancy through to adulthood. Cognitive skills are the skills underpinning flexible problem-solving and effective learning: attention, memory, flexible thinking, speed of information processing and language. These skills underpin a child's learning, social and emotional development (McLean, 2016b).

Developmental differences in cognitive functioning

The literature on the impact of early adversity on brain development is now quite large and still growing. Much of this literature talks about brain development in the context of trauma; however there is growing recognition that there are other forms of early adversity that also affect brain development. For example, we now recognize that prenatal exposure to alcohol and other substances is also common amongst children in care Prenatal exposure to alcohol is associated with sensory, learning, behavioural and social difficulties in children (Chapters 4–7 have more information about these developmental differences). We also know that children who enter care are likely to have been exposed to a wide range of early life adversity – including dislocation, neglect, poverty and chronic family stress – and that these experiences affect foundational cognitive skills in ways we don't yet fully understand.

The areas of development that are affected by early adversity include language development, sensory integration, and the development of memory and organization skills (executive functioning). These are the areas of developmental difference that are addressed in this book (see Box 2 for detail on research in this area).

Why focus on developmental differences?

In this book, I take a 'trans-diagnostic' approach to supporting children. What does this mean? Put simply, it means that I try to 'look beyond' whatever diagnosis the child has been given. The developmental differences discussed in this book are those that are commonly associated with 1) children who have experienced complex trauma and life adversities but also 2) children with mental health diagnoses that are associated with challenging behaviour, such as attention deficit hyperactivity disorder (ADHD), autism, fetal alcohol spectrum disorder (FASD) or conduct disorder. The book focuses on the developmental differences in brain functioning that are common across these groups of children. This is why I'd describe this approach as trans-diagnostic. I ask 'What's different for this child?', rather than 'What's wrong with this child?' and focus on supporting and strengthening the areas of functioning that are underdeveloped due to early adversity. This approach provides a means for addressing challenging behaviour and learning difficulties in a positive way.

Developmental differences reflect the important ways in which your child's experience of the world *differs* from young people without a history of early adversity. You can support your child by understanding their unique developmental differences and learning to respond according to their needs. Your child's developmental differences reflect delays in different aspects of cognitive functioning that we should strive to *understand and accommodate.* Over time, we should aim to help a child to develop the skills to manage and cope with their unique differences.

Developmental differences and the development of behaviour problems

It is my view that many of the behaviour difficulties and failures young people experience are due to the chronic 'mismatch' between their underlying needs (developmental differences) and societal expectations; rather than being due to their developmental differences *per se.* Many behavioural and social difficulties develop because young people are living in a world that is not well suited to children with developmental differences.

What do I mean by this? Let's consider a child with a physical disability; for example, their legs aren't strong so they need a wheelchair to get around. We wouldn't expect a child who is in a wheelchair to have to climb stairs. We modify their world so that they have a different way of getting to the top of the stairs – by installing a ramp or a lift. We wouldn't expect a visually impaired person to read a newspaper without modifying the environment to enable them to see more clearly – by supplying a magnification lens or large print material.

These are two examples in which we clearly understand the need to modify the environment, and adjust our expectations, to suit a child's current ability. Climbing stairs or reading unassisted is impossible; it's beyond their current ability. Even if such a child is willing to climb stairs, or read unassisted, they cannot experience success. Their ability is unrelated to their motivation. It has nothing to do with laziness; it's just their current ability. We are happy to adjust our expectations and modify the environment to accommodate a child's physical difference.

We would probably be met with angry protest if we were to insist that a person try to do what is beyond their ability or their current functioning. Yet we expect children to comply with our requests, often without stopping to consider whether they are actually capable or whether the task is beyond their current ability.

One important message of this book is that we can avoid a lot of frustration and behaviour difficulties in young people when we really stop and consider their ability to comply. Children may not be able to meet our expectations because they have significant compromises that mean they may be functioning at a much younger developmental stage. As Diane Malbin (*Trying Differently Rather Than Harder*, 2002, p.16) says: 'It's not that they *won't*…it's that they possibly *can't*.'

If we can identify and accept the developmental difference underpinning a child's behaviour, we begin to put our energy into thinking about how to make the world more accessible to them. With this change in mindset, we start to think about children's behaviour in terms of a chronic 'mismatch' between children's developmental differences and the expectations placed on them by society.

This is a very different way to think about children's behaviour. But this shift in mindset helps orient our thinking away from 'What's wrong with you?' and starts us asking questions like 'What's different for you?', 'What are you trying to tell me?' and 'What do I need to do differently in order for you to be successful?'

To avoid unnecessary battles, we need to meet a child at their current level of development. We need to adjust our expectations and modify their world in order to help them to succeed. We need to understand that their behaviour is a form of communication – it's letting you know just how 'out of their depth' they feel. We need to support their development in areas of delay and explicitly teach them the skills they need to know to relinquish challenging behaviour.

This book is intended as a guide for foster and adoptive parents who may be struggling to understand the best way to support their child. Using a 'trans-diagnostic' approach I focus on the developmental differences underpinning behaviour disorders and on the growing evidence base about how to respond so that behaviour issues are minimized.

BOX 2

Research linking early adversity to developmental differences in cognitive functioning

This section summarizes the evidence linking early adversity with developmental difference. This is a rapidly developing field. Researchers don't yet fully understand the mechanisms and pathways by which early adversity affects brain development. There's no need to read this section at all – you can just skip this and work through the rest of the book. However, I've provided a sample of references for those of you who want to learn more.

Children who are fostered or adopted from care are likely to have experienced a range of early life adversities, including trauma, abuse, neglect and antenatal substance exposure. We know that behavioural and mental health issues are more common amongst children in care than in children from similar backgrounds who are not placed in care (Ford et al. 2007; Luke et al. 2014). We also now know that adverse childhood experiences can be associated with the development of poor physical and mental health outcomes in adulthood (Anda, Felitti and Bremner, 2006; Price-Robertson, Higgins and Vassallo, 2013).

There has been a lot written about the effects that prolonged exposure to stress and trauma is thought to have on brain development (see Atkinson, 2013; Cook et al., 2005; Perry, 2006, 2009; Van der Kolk et al., 2009). Different forms of early adversity such as alcohol and substance exposure in utero, placement instability, poverty, neglect and pervasive developmental issues also affect children's development (De Jong, 2010; McLean and McDougall, 2014; Zilberstein and Popper, 2014).

Researchers use a variety of techniques to examine the relationship between childhood adversity and cognitive development, and use these approaches to infer how brain development has been affected. These techniques include brain scanning, measurement of the hormones related to brain activity, and measures of brain performance during specific cognitive activities (for reviews of neuroimaging and neuropsychological studies see McCrory, De Brito and Viding, 2010; McCrory et al., 2011).

While these researchers tend to agree that early life adversity affects the brain development and stress hormones, the exact nature of this change and how it occurs is still being debated (Frodl and O'Keane, 2013; McCrory et al., 2010; McEwen, 2012; McLean, 2016b). So while we can agree that brain development is affected by early adversity, we can't yet be sure exactly how this occurs and which children might be more vulnerable (McCrory et al., 2010; McCrory et al., 2011; McLaughlin, Sheridan and Lambert, 2014; McLean, 2016b; Teicher, Anderson and Polcari, 2012). We are much more certain about the link between exposure to alcohol and other substances in the womb and later cognitive, language and sensory difficulties (see McLean and McDougall, 2014; McLean, McDougall and Russell, 2014); although here again we are yet to understand why some children are more affected than others.

On the whole, however, there is enough research to suggest that children who have experienced or witnessed violence, trauma, abuse or neglect, or those exposed to toxins in utero do experience a range of developmental differences (McCrory et al., 2011; McLaughlin et al., 2014; McLean, 2016b: McLean and McDougall, 2014). Some of the main developmental differences include:

- Delays in cognitive and social milestones (see Chapter 2: De Bellis et al., 2009; Hart and Rubia, 2012; Hildyard and Wolfe, 2002; Koenen et al., 2003; McLaughlin et al., 2014; Prasad, Kramer and Ewing Cobbs, 2005; Pollak et al., 2010)

- Difficulty in regulating the sensory world (see Chapter 4: Cascio, 2010; Cermak and Groza, 1998; Franklin et al., 2008)

- Difficulty in understanding, communicating and language delay (see Chapter 5: Grant and Gravestock, 2003; Sylvestre, Bussières and Bouchard, 2016; Wyper and Rasmussen, 2011)

- Difficulty in emotional regulation (see Chapter 6: Dvir *et al.*, 2014; Kuo *et al.*, 2015)

- Difficulty with executive control, memory and organization (see Chapter 7: Carrion *et al.*, 2010; Cicchetti *et al.*, 2010; De Bellis *et al.*, 2002; DePrince, Weinzierl and Combs, 2009; Hart and Rubia, 2012; Teicher *et al.*, 2012; Moradi *et al.*,1999; Nolin and Ethier, 2007)

- Differences (bias) in social information processing (see Chapter 8: De Brito *et al.*, 2013; Kelly *et al.*, 2013; McCrory, Gerin and Viding, 2017; McLaughlin *et al.*, 2014; Pollak and Sinha, 2002).

(For more information on this topic, see also Cook *et al.*, 2005; De Lisi and Vaughn, 2011; Lansdown, Burnell and Allen, 2007; McCrory *et al.*, 2010; McLean, 2016b; McLean and McDougall, 2014; Noll *et al.*, 2006; Ogilvie *et al.*, 2011; Perry and Dobson, 2013.)

Each of these areas of developmental difference is explored in more detail in this book.

As we've discussed, many behavioural difficulties are underpinned by developmental differences and working with, not against, developmental differences will support your child's development. We'll talk about how to identify and address these developmental differences a little later in this book. In the next chapter, I give a summary of some of the general developmental milestones for children at different ages.

Chapter 2

An Introduction to Normal Development

Identifying developmental delays

In this chapter, we review the normal developmental trends and developmental milestones. I've included these as a guide to determining when your child might be falling behind; you may need to consider whether there are developmental differences that might be contributing to this. These 'milestones' can be thought of as benchmarks; and reflect the kinds of things a child should be mastering at each developmental age and stage. I've included this chapter because foster and adoptive parents often ask how they can know if their child's development is on track.

As we'll emphasize in this book, many behaviour problems are caused by a child's frustration due to underlying developmental differences. Understanding your child's current developmental functioning is important. The information included in this chapter is not intended to be exhaustive, but it is detailed enough to give you a quick reference point. It can help you determine if further professional support might be warranted and act as a 'conversation starter' with your child's caseworker.

If, after reading this chapter, you are concerned about your child's development, you might like to discuss this chapter with a doctor or developmental psychologist. Although I don't cover infancy, I've included links to information about normal development in this age group at the end of the book. In this chapter, I've attempted to separate what you would expect for your child's cognitive, language and social development at each age.

A guide to your child's development from age three to five years

Your child's thinking

It is normal for children at this age to be egocentric in their thinking. This means that they have trouble taking another person's perspective and they truly believe that the world revolves around them and their needs. Their thinking is 'magical' rather than logical. Their world is full of imagination and fantasy, but they can have real difficulty in separating fantasy from reality. All this means that they can have wonderful imagination, believing everything they wish for becomes real.

It is normal for children at this age to think that they can control their world by their thoughts – that what they think comes true because they have made it happen by thinking it. They believe that everything they wish for becomes real. If something bad happens, however, they are likely to automatically believe that it is because they somehow wished it to happen; this is related to their magical thinking. For this reason, children are very likely to blame themselves for any loss or trauma that occurs during this phase of their development.

Your child's language and communication

By this stage your child will normally be able to use four- to five-word sentences and repeat up to four digits back to you. By the end of this developmental period your child should be able to use language to make requests. They should be able to relate simple narratives and use future tense in their narratives. They should be easily understood by most people, including strangers. Their descriptive language should include a growing range of descriptive words; they should be able to name at least four colours. Your child should be able to use pronouns such as 'I', 'we, 'me' and 'you' correctly, and count to ten or more. They will be able to give their full name and are likely to be able to give their full address (but this may depend on how long they have been living with you and how many other addresses they have lived at).

Your child's social development

During this time your child will begin to be curious about the difference between boys and girls, and between a boy's and a girl's anatomy. Your child's friendships at this age are opportunistic and based around joint activities. Because of your child's egocentric thinking and genuine difficulty in seeing things from another's perspective, they can experience frustration with their playmates, and engage in behaviour that can seem selfish to others.

A child at this age should be starting to develop a moral conscience. Towards the end of this stage of development they should start to feel guilty when they are disobedient due to their emerging understanding of right and wrong. Most of the time, however, it is normal for children at this stage to need an adult present to remind them of what is right and what is wrong. If left to their own devices, it is normal for children of this age to 'forget' to do the right thing.

By the end of this stage we would also expect a child to begin to consistently show concern for a friend who is hurt or asks for help. By the end of this stage we would expect a child to show a wide range of emotions. We would expect them to cry when distressed (e.g. when physically injured), showing they are confident that an adult will comfort them when hurt. At the end of this stage they should begin to show a little more independence, being relatively well able to tolerate some separation from their caregiver. During this stage of development it is entirely normal for children to show fear of the dark, fear of animals and fear of dying (due to an emerging understanding of permanence).

Your child's skill development

By the end of this period of development your child should be able to dress and undress without help most of the time (they may still need some support with buttons, etc.) and they may attempt to tie their shoelaces. A child of this age should be toilet trained but may still wet the bed on occasion. At this age a child can swing, climb stairs, hop on one foot and ride a tricycle (or bike with trainer wheels). They will be able to catch a bounced ball most of the time. Their fine motor skills are rapidly developing at this age and they will be able to hold a pencil, cut along a line and draw people with at least four 'parts'.

When should I consider professional support?

You may want to consider seeking further support if your child hasn't met most of the normal developmental milestones outlined here. If your child does not communicate or is not understood by others, you should seek support from a speech pathologist. If they do not show interest in social interaction or interactive games, you may also be referred to a psychologist to rule out pervasive developmental disorders like autism spectrum disorder (ASD). If your child is over four years of age and cannot grasp a crayon between thumb and fingers, cannot understand a two-part command (e.g. pick up the cup and put it on the table) or is unable to concentrate on a single activity for more than five minutes, then a referral to an occupational therapist and psychologist may be warranted. Any sudden loss of previously acquired skills, such as self-care, toileting or eating skills, or sudden regression (increased fear of separation, sudden onset of night terrors) should be investigated further by an appropriate professional.

A guide to your child's development from age five to seven years

Your child's thinking

Children at this age are more reliably able to differentiate what's real from what's imaginary, although they will still enjoy 'make believe' play. Make believe play may become more elaborate; for example, a child might allocate roles to themselves and their friends and act out characters from books, television or movies.

Children's thinking at this stage is less 'magical' and they become more aware of the permanence of death and loss, although they may revert to 'magical' and 'wishful' thinking under pressure (for example, they may retain a 'fantasy' about being reunited with their biological family). They begin to see themselves as people with a range of personal strengths and weaknesses. They begin to describe themselves less in concrete (black and white) terms (e.g. I run really fast) and begin to describe themselves in dimensional terms (e.g. I'm the best runner but I'm not the best at drawing).

Children during this stage become more interested in friendships and begin to understand that not everyone sees the world in the same way that they do. They start to become more prosocial – more cooperative and interested in helping others. A child of this age will normally agree to follow most social and household rules, although they might expect to have input about the 'fairness' of rules and the order in which household tasks are done.

Your child's language and communication

Children at this age will use their language in increasingly social ways. It is normal at this stage for your child to use their developing language to drive and master social interactions, rather than using their language to demand things or to comment on their own interests. They will start to use language to learn about others. It is common for them to question others about their activities and lives.

They will be able to reliably count to ten or more (typically up to 100); they can use language to talk about the future and know the names of most colours. Their sentences are increasingly complex and they typically use seven or more words in a sentence. They enjoy using language skills to sing and act out roles and typically show an interest in recognizing words and language in books and in the wider world (for example, they enjoy reading shop windows and street signs).

Your child's social development

This stage of development is marked by children moving from an egocentric (the child believes the world revolves around them and is unable to see things from another's perspective) to a more socially oriented 'world view'. Children at this age are increasingly interested in friendship; they want to be like their friends and they can usually name at least one or two friends at any one time. Friendship is important to a child of this age, but it is not uncommon for friendship groups to change frequently. Socially, they are less likely to be involved in explosive disputes with friends; they start to understand that others feel differently to them, although they may not really understand why.

With this increasing ability to take another's perspective they begin to be better at sharing and cooperative games, understanding the need to take turns. This 'understanding' may break down under pressure, and it will still be important to provide supervision, structure and support for a child of this age with cooperative play (for example, they may need reminding to put away their precious toys and only leave out the toys they are willing to share with friends).

A child of this age will begin to develop a sense of their own 'conscience'; they begin to be influenced by their internal sense of right or wrong. It is normal for a child of this age to need caregiver support sometimes to co-regulate (manage) strong emotions and to reliably demonstrate cooperative behaviour. Children at this age begin to adopt and act out gender roles.

Your child's skill development

This age is marked by a rapid increase in your child's physical and fine motor skills. Entry to school means increased expectations for fine motor control and concentration. These expectations can act as a stimulus for rapid skill development but they can also add to the frustration of children who are experiencing developmental delays. We would generally expect children of this age group to care for their own toileting and feeding needs. They can hop, skip and stand on one foot reliably. They will be able to print some letters, will begin to be able to read and should show a clear understanding of the correspondence between letters and sounds.

When should I consider professional support?

You may want to consider seeking further support if your child hasn't met most of the normal developmental milestones outlined here. This is an age where learning difficulties and difficulty in emotional regulation start to emerge, with the increase in social and learning expectations introduced in the school environment.

During this age we might see the development of persistent fears or continuing difficulty in separating from a caregiver. Any persistent fears should be explored. We might expect some fear in children with abuse backgrounds; however, it may indicate the need for psychological intervention and support to prevent the development of more entrenched difficulties. Any sudden loss of previously acquired skills, such as self-care, toileting or eating skills, or sudden regression (increased fear of separation, sudden onset of night terrors) should be investigated further by an appropriate professional.

A guide to your child's development from age seven to twelve years

Your child's thinking

At this stage of development, children are reliably able to see things from another's point of view; they have developed and demonstrate genuine empathy for others. Children at this stage know the difference between fantasy and reality. They increasingly rely on logic, abstract thinking (ability to think about ideas and concepts) and verbal skills to resolve differences of opinion without resorting to violence.

During this stage any developmental differences and delays in cognitive functioning or language skills will be frustrating for them. Delays in these areas mean that your child is not equipped with the same problem-solving 'currency' as other children. In this case, they may come to be viewed as the cause of conflict and friendship issues.

Although children are increasingly logical at this age, it is still normal for your child to need support with organization and routines. Your child will be able to engage in more sophisticated and complex conversations during this phase of development, particularly around their areas of interest. They develop an understanding of the passage of time and show increasing competence and mastery in their areas of interest, and in literacy, numeracy and computing.

This is a stage of development when your child's individual strengths begin to emerge and can be supported. You may notice your child 'distance' themselves from childish ways of thinking and behaving. Towards the end of this developmental stage (at nine to twelve years) children become much more logical and 'grown up' in their thinking. They often become intolerant of younger children, 'magical' thinking and the activities they found enjoyable as a younger child. They become more interested in facts and general knowledge; have a strong need to experience success and mastery (fixing things, learning facts, demonstrating knowledge to others); and begin to understand and apply abstract concepts like space and dimensions.

Your child's language and communication

By the end of this stage a child has learned how to use language to reliably get their needs met. They are able to use language and reasoning skills to solve most social difficulties and problems. They may also increasingly use language to identify their peer group, their interests and to show their knowledge to others. During this age, children's developing access to literacy and their developing knowledge of emotional vocabulary mean they may enjoy using journals and other expressive means of managing emotionally demanding situations.

Your child's social development

Children's social development during this stage normally centres on maintaining their peer group and following their interests. During this age, they are likely to become interested in a hobby or sporting activity, and are usually willing to join in with club activities centred on their interests.

Their friendship groups are normally still gender based but they may start to socialize more with the opposite gender where this revolves around a common interest. While the peer group is important, it is usual for children in this stage to have intense and exclusive 'best friend' relationships, usually with a same-sex child. While their family remains important to them, during this stage of development they increasingly base their identity on their peer or friendship group, which is usually based on similar interests. Towards the end of this stage of development, your child will firmly identify with a peer group and the influence of their friends and peers starts to become stronger, although adults remain important role models to them.

During this phase of development, children begin to reliably show an internalized sense of conscience in which their sense of right and wrong becomes part of their own values, and they aren't as reliant on adults to reinforce rules. Socially, this is often reflected in a focus on concepts of fairness, and children during this stage can show the ability to place the needs of others over their own. They are able at this age to reliably tell the difference between bad behaviour and bad intentions. This means they are able to determine when someone deliberately hurts them versus when this happens by accident, although children who have experienced intentional harm from adults in the past may continue to struggle with this distinction.

This is an age where there is increasing interest in gender roles, pregnancy, sex and babies. Children at this age are increasingly aware of the differences in gender roles and the physical differences between boys and girls. They may ask basic questions about reproduction and ask about the meaning of swear words. Towards the end of this developmental period, it is normal for children to experiment with 'boyfriend/girlfriend' relationships, or play games like truth or dare with a mild 'sexual' component to them.

Your child's skill development

Children at this age are driven by a desire for mastery and skill development. They enjoy their growing sense of competence and may focus their interests on activities where they enjoy success. They are increasingly able to tolerate failure and losing in competitive situations, but may still need support with this. During this time, marked differences in body growth and the onset of puberty can make children feel more awkward and challenge their confidence. They are increasingly interested in opportunities to demonstrate their competence outside their family (for example, in school or in sporting clubs).

When should I consider professional support?

You may want to consider seeking further support if your child hasn't met most of the normal developmental milestones outlined here. During this age we might see a persistence in the dependence and reliance of earlier stages, and friendship issues might emerge if your child is having difficulty with problem solving or in accurately identifying the intentions of others. Children can rapidly lose confidence and self-esteem if academic difficulties are not picked up and addressed early.

Persistent difficulties such as your child seeming preoccupied, easily frustrated, emotional or over-reliant on adults may indicate the need for psychological intervention and support to prevent the development of more entrenched difficulties. Any sudden loss of previously acquired skills, such as self-care, toileting or eating skills, or sudden regression (increased difficulty with separation, sudden onset of nightmares) should be investigated further by an appropriate professional.

A guide to your child's development in adolescence (age twelve+)
Your child's thinking

Children at this stage are reliably able to take another's perspective and can think both logically and abstractly about problems. Many adolescents undertake a prolonged period of self-reflection during this stage of development, examining, comparing and contrasting their beliefs and values against those of their parents and other significant adults. They may develop and test out their emerging values, beliefs and 'identity' through argument with adults and other significant adults. It is normal for your child to question their origins, how they came to be placed in foster or adoptive care, and to be preoccupied with their similarity and difference to people in their family of origin.

Your child's social development

During this phase your child may return to having a wider and mixed group of friends. Teenagers usually demonstrate a strong sense of morals and right and wrong and compliance with social norms. Older adolescents may make choices based on their unique view of what is morally right, which can on occasion conflict with legal definitions of right and wrong.

At the same time, during this phase there is a return to their earlier egocentric thinking – teenagers typically think that they are the centre of others' thoughts and attention – leading to self-consciousness. It is normal for teenagers to become intensely self-focused (self-centred and concerned about their body image and appearance).

Your child's social identity is increasingly important and they begin to define themselves by their interests outside their family. Their friendships will increasingly be based not only on interests but on loyalty, trust and self-revelation; and they are able to make conscious choices about who to trust (although this may need to be learned over time).

During this stage your child's physical body is undergoing massive change and development. This corresponds with a surge of hormones that will make any otherwise rational child emotionally volatile and argumentative. The physical changes of puberty begin if they have not already and they may become sexually active during this time. During this stage children begin the long process of defining themselves; this is a normal part of 'experimenting' with being an emerging adult. During this stage children will alternate rapidly between being fiercely independent and needing the comfort, nurturing and support of a younger child. The key questions of adolescents are 'Who am I?' and 'Where do I belong?' Adolescence is a time of questioning, reflection and high emotionality. There is an increased need for sleep and there is an increased risk of sleep disorders developing during this stage. A young person's social presentation and social 'identity' become increasingly important during this time. Your child is likely to show a renewed interest in their family of origin due to their developing self-identity.

Your child's language and communication

Young people's developing language, ability to use language abstractly and interest in the popular culture of language will mean that they experiment with language, music and art as part of their identity formation. They may identify with a language 'subculture', using language to define their likes, interests and values.

Your child's skill development

Young people at this age are increasingly interested in making their own decisions and learning from their own mistakes. The main skills of interest to adolescents are those related to their emerging sense of emotional, social and physical independence. They may develop skills of independent living and show interest in learning to drive or working outside the home.

When should I consider professional support?

You may want to consider seeking further support if your child hasn't met most of the normal developmental milestones outlined here. During this age we might see persistent difficulty with managing intense emotions and mood swings. Friendship issues might emerge because your child may have moved schools frequently or may not have the language and cognitive ability required to be socially skilled.

If your child has developed unrealistic expectations of themselves (retreating to fantasy), has an unrealistic sense of self-importance or has low sense of mastery and self-esteem, it is worth pursuing professional assistance. It is extremely common for adolescents to develop behavioural and emotional difficulties as they work through their sense of identity and belonging, and it is common to need professional support during this time irrespective of how long your child has been with you. Any sudden loss of previously acquired skills, such as self-care, or sudden regression in behaviour or sleep should be investigated further by an appropriate professional.

Remember the information provided in this chapter is intended as a starting point for considering the normal developmental milestones that a child must master during their development. When a child has developmental difference each stage of development is more difficult. When children start to fall behind their peers they experience frustration, low self-esteem and shame. Identifying, understanding and supporting their developmental differences are important in re-directing your child towards a normal developmental pathway.

Chapter 3

An Introduction to the Reasons for Challenging Behaviour

I'd like to introduce you to an approach to understanding and responding to children's behaviour. It's based on a simple assumption – that all children's behaviour is a form of communication.

Behaviour 'management' is most effective when we have a good understanding about what message a child's behaviour is sending – we need to understand the 'language' of their behaviour. When the message behind the behaviour becomes clear it is much easier to address. In this chapter we'll discuss some of the most common messages that behaviour communicates. We'll unpack the 'language' of challenging behaviour and strategies to support your child to develop a more socially acceptable 'language' for communicating their needs to you.

Let's take an example that will help illustrate this point. Imagine you are magically transported to a foreign country where everyone is speaking in another language. You know you will need to learn the language in order to get your needs met and to make friends, but initially you have no idea what people are trying to tell you!

When a child is placed in your home they can have the same experience. They need to learn your 'language', customs and culture. Your home can be just like a 'foreign country' to them, and they can't understand how to make themselves understood in your 'language'.

At the same time, you will also find your adoptive or foster child's language strange and unfamiliar. You will need to learn their language. For a child with developmental difference and special needs, this language often includes behaviour. Learning to speak your child's language will take time and you will make mistakes (just like you do when you learn any foreign language).

In this chapter, we'll explore how to 'interpret' children's behaviour. It is important to understand the message your child is trying to communicate through their challenging behaviour. As we'll see, your child's behaviour conveys important messages about what they need from you. This chapter will give you an introduction to 'translating' your child's language so that you can help them to meet their needs in other ways.

What is challenging behaviour and when does your child need professional support?

All children will have challenging behaviour from time to time. However, most of the time this behaviour doesn't reach the level or intensity that affects a child's ability to take part in social, educational, family or community activities.

We typically define 'challenging behaviour' as behaviour that is *at odds with 'cultural/social' expectations*; and that occurs at a *level, intensity and duration* that *precludes a child from accessing normal social, educational and community activities*. In other words, a behaviour becomes problematic when it limits a child's access to normal activities or results in social exclusion or danger to self and others and it then needs to be addressed (see *Challenging Behaviour: Analysis and Intervention in People with Learning Disabilities* by Eric Emerson).

If you think your child's behaviour falls into this category, it will be important to work out a plan to address it using the guiding principles and guiding questions in this chapter. I'm sure that as a foster or adoptive parent you have received plenty of advice about how to manage your child's behaviour. Keep in mind, *you* are the one who has to live with the approach you take, not others. You need to be comfortable with the approach you choose. Your approach must include steps to meet your child's underlying need.

Most importantly, the approach you use must strengthen your relationship with your child, not damage it. There is absolutely nothing to be gained from getting a child's compliance when it occurs at the expense of your child's well-being and their bond with you. Punishments and penalties are not effective in the longer term because they do absolutely nothing to *teach the skills and behaviours* that your child needs to succeed. Punishment can be effective in teaching a child *what not to do* but does not give them the skills and knowledge to know *what to do.*

After reading this book you may still need to seek professional support, especially when the behaviour you are dealing with places your child or others in danger. This chapter will still be a good place to start, even if you do need to seek professional support. The information here will provide you with useful insights that you can discuss further with a trained behaviour specialist.

So let's start with some of the guiding principles for supporting children and families affected by challenging behaviour.

Ask yourself: is this a rule or an expectation?

Decide what kind of behaviour transgression you are dealing with. Be clear about the difference between your *rules* and your *expectations* (*Children and Residential Experiences: Creating Conditions for Change* by Martha J. Holden is useful further reading on this). The difference between these is explained in Box 3. Behaviour 'rules' should be directly related to safety in the home, school or community. An example of a rule for a four-year-old child might be to 'hold an adult's hand when crossing the road'. It's a non-negotiable, safety-related behaviour that you *absolutely must ensure your child understands and complies with.*

There shouldn't really be too many rules. I expect that there are only a handful or so of absolutely non-negotiable behaviour rules that relate to the safety of your child and others. Take a moment now to think about what these rules might be.

We can contrast these with your behavioural *expectations* for your child. Behavioural expectations might be more related to polite social conventions, paying attention to task, social cooperation or daily chores. These are behaviours that you *desire* from your child. These are behaviours, however, that they – because of their early adversity and family background – *may not yet have had the opportunity to learn*. It's the kind of behaviour we'd like from them, but that we realize might take time, support and guidance for them to achieve.

So the first principle is to decide what kind of behaviour you are dealing with – a non-negotiable *rule* or a behavioural *expectation*. The answer to this question will determine the urgency with which you address your child's behaviours (see Box 3).

BOX 3

Are you arguing about a safety rule or a behavioural expectation?

Before addressing any behavioural issues with your child, it is important to consider whether or not the behaviour concerned is really worth taking on at this time. How do we do this? The very first place to start is in deciding whether or not this is a behaviour you have to take on. Ask yourself the following questions:

- Is this behaviour something that puts my child, my family or others at risk?

- Is this something I don't want to have to negotiate on?

- Is this an argument I must win?

If the answer to these questions is yes, it's likely the behaviour you are thinking of is a safety rule. Safety rules refer to behaviours that are non-negotiable because they affect the physical safety of your child, yourself or others.

In addressing safety-related behaviours, the first step is determining whether or not your child doesn't know any better (your child isn't able to because they lack the knowledge about how to comply) or whether they are willing and able to comply.

Let's take the example of running across the road without looking or holding an adult's hand. I think we'd all agree that crossing the road safely is a safety rule.

- A child may not know any better; they may never have been taught how to cross a road safely. They may be willing to behave, but just not know what is expected.

- They may know how to but choose not to comply.

The implications are different in each case.

If your child is deliberately non-compliant despite knowing how to comply, you must state the rule and win the battle. This might involve noticing each step towards doing the right thing (for example, standing next to an adult, holding an adult's hand, walking alongside an adult, etc.).

Your child may not know the rules of crossing the road. In this case you will need to spell out what is expected and notice each time your child tries to do the right thing (complies or attempts to comply with your rule).

But the bottom line is, there are behaviours that you simply cannot ignore.

In contrast, almost all other behaviours relate to expectations – they are behaviours that you'd like your child to comply with, but where non-compliance won't affect their safety or others' safety.

While safety rules are non-negotiable, all other behavioural expectations are best viewed as reflecting our *aspirations* for a child's behaviour – behaviours that the child can work towards being able to accomplish over time.

An example of a safety behaviour might be 'Always walk on the footpath'; whereas an example of a behavioural expectation might be 'We always say please and thank you.'

When children have come from abusive, neglectful or socially deprived backgrounds, they may not yet have had the opportunity to develop the behaviours we would like. We need to adjust our expectations, provide emotional support, and teach them the 'missing' skills needed to meet our expectations .

Ask yourself: is this the most important thing to take on right now?

In other words, *choose your battle*. The decision about which behaviour to focus on and which to selectively ignore is very important. Behaviour change is most effective when we focus on only one behaviour at a time.

Always prioritize behaviours that involve the violation of a safety rule and place your child or others at risk (see the first principle above). If this is the case, state the safety rule clearly to the child. Make sure you tell them *what you want them to do* (rather than what you don't want them to do). For example, 'We always hold an adult's hand when we cross the road' or 'Wait for an adult', rather than 'Don't cross the road by yourself!'

If the difficulties relate to behavioural expectations, then you will need to decide which of these behaviours to address first. Prioritize those behaviours that, when addressed, will improve your child's relationship with you and their social opportunities. Ask yourself, 'What would be different for my child if this behaviour didn't exist?' Ask yourself, 'What does my child need in order to relinquish this behaviour?' (More on this later.)

Ask yourself: have I involved my child in setting behavioural goals?

Ensure you *involve your child* in setting goals that concern their behaviour. Involve your child in creating solutions that will work for them. Make sure your child understands what behaviour you will be supporting them with and why. Make sure you use age appropriate and simple language; for example, 'We are going to practise what you can do when you're feeling angry.' If you involve your child in discussions about learning to manage tricky behaviour, you will give them a more concrete understanding of what the 'end goal' is. This often results in much more creative and child-led solutions that children truly 'own'. Both parents need to use the same child-friendly language to describe the issue you will be addressing – for example, 'when angry feelings come along' or 'when you get a sick tummy'. Make sure you both have a shared understanding about what behaviour needs to change and why.

Ask yourself: do I understand what message this behaviour is communicating to me?

Take the time to really *understand what this behaviour is communicating* to you. You can be sure that any unwanted behaviour has been an important way for your child to cope and get their needs met. Your child will find it difficult to give up a behaviour unless you are able to provide them with an alternative way to meet their needs. Ask yourself, 'What message is my child sending with this behaviour?'; 'What purpose does this behaviour serve for my child?'; 'What's different for my child?' and 'What does my child need instead, in order to let go of this behaviour?' Many children have good insight into their behaviour and the feelings that go with it. We'll look at some of the needs that are communicated by challenging behaviour later in this chapter.

Ask yourself: am I making a habit of noticing how things have improved?

Notice and celebrate the small wins with your child. Consider what you can do to reward yourself on a regular basis for 'hanging in there'. It can be exhausting to deal with challenging behaviour on a daily basis. Many behaviour issues take time to resolve. Some behaviours will diminish but re-emerge during times of stress. Your attitude will make all the difference; it is important for you to find a way to notice the small gains and incremental progress. Sometimes it is only when you look back that you realize how far you and your child have come.

Set-backs and 'regression' to old behaviours at times of stress are normal. Stressors such as significant anniversaries, the placement of another child, issues in your child's family of origin, changes of school and the onset of puberty are all common triggers for a regression to old behaviours.

BOX 4

Five principles for addressing challenging behaviour

- Decide if you are dealing with a safety rule or an expectation.

- Choose your 'battle'.

- Involve your child in setting goals and creating solutions.

- Focus only on what your child's behaviour is communicating to you.

- Notice the small changes and celebrate success.

Challenging behaviours and their reasons

The main message of this chapter is that children's behaviour is meaningful even if it is sometimes perplexing (if we don't yet understand their 'language'). The remainder of this chapter will help you to decide what purpose your child's behaviour serves and what their behaviour might be communicating to you.

While reading the following, I encourage you to keep in mind a current behaviour you may be dealing with. Take a moment to reflect on the following:

- What happens as a result of this behaviour?

- What does my child avoid because of this behaviour?

- What does my child gain?

- In what situations does this behaviour occur?

- What's different about the times my child doesn't' show this behaviour?

It might be useful to write this information down before moving on.

It would also be useful to consider the following as you work through this chapter:

- Does my child have the skills and coping mechanisms needed to let go of this behaviour?

- Is it that my child *doesn't want to comply* or just that my child *isn't yet able to*?

In my experience, there are a few common reasons for challenging behaviour amongst children in care. These include:

- Feeling afraid or unsafe. (The behaviour is a safety behaviour.)

- Needing to manage or control important relationships. (The behaviour is about managing personal boundaries.)

- Regulating the emotional and sensory world. (The behaviour is about self-regulation – the child is trying to self-soothe.)

- Lack of skill to respond in a fast and complex world. (The behaviour is about delayed skills and abilities.)

Each of these types of behaviour communicates a different message to us.

We'll now explore each of these reasons for challenging behaviour. We'll consider how to tell which type of behaviour is relevant for your child. Later in this book, we'll look at the last two types of behaviour in much more detail: behaviours that are related to regulating the sensory and emotional world and behaviours that are related to delays in cognitive and language functioning. Let's look at each of the four behaviour types next.

Safety behaviours

A safety behaviour is a one that occurs when your child is trying to avoid feeling vulnerable or afraid. The hallmark feature of safety behaviour is that this behaviour means your child does not need to experience overwhelming feelings of shame, humiliation or fear. Your child will almost invariably feel better as a result of engaging in this behaviour – safer, calmer and less anxious.

The core driver of your child's behaviour is to defend against overwhelming fear or shame.

The key messages your child is communicating to you through this behaviour are:

- I'm afraid.

- I'm ashamed.

- I don't like this.

- And I don't know how else to tell you!

Safety behaviours are powerful. The result of engaging in safety behaviour is that your child avoids bad feelings of fear and shame *and* feels much better very quickly, as a direct result of engaging in these avoidance behaviours. For this reason, safety behaviours are extremely effective and rewarding behaviours. They make your child feel better very quickly.

Safety behaviours aren't necessarily about your child's physical safety. Your child does not have to be in *actual* danger to exhibit safety behaviours. They can feel afraid even if, objectively, we know they are actually in no danger at all. It's your child's *perception* that drives safety behaviours.

Safety behaviours can occur in response to reminders of past trauma or in response to reminders of past shame and humiliation – both are common and familiar emotions to a child who has experienced abuse or neglect. Safety behaviours occur when your child anticipates and tries to avoid situations, people or activities that risk them *re-experiencing* strong and terrifying emotions – terror, fear, shame or humiliation – in the here and now.

The core purpose of safety behaviour is to escape actual or anticipated unpleasant feelings. For this reason it is powerfully rewarding behaviour and can take time to diminish.

Safety behaviour can also occur in response to trauma triggers (reminders of past traumatic events and abuse). These behaviours appear – at first – to happen 'out of the blue' and without warning. Through careful observation you will notice the behaviour occurs in response to one or more aspects of your child's surroundings – it could be one or more sights, smells, sensations or sounds – that remind your child of a past trauma or shameful humiliation. If your child has been traumatized in the past, any aspect of their surroundings that is similar enough to the physical and sensory surroundings in which the original trauma occurred can trigger a re-experiencing of overwhelming fear and a survival response.

Safety behaviours can take the form of a primitive fight, flight or freeze response. Therefore the behaviours usually involve anger and lashing out (fight), running away or other avoidance (flight) or mentally removing themselves (tuning out, blanking out, 'blackouts', dissociating – detaching from awareness and emotions). A child may have very little recollection of their behaviour after this kind of response.

Safety behaviours can also be less extreme avoidance behaviours that the child uses when they anticipate embarrassment and shame, anger or apprehension. These can occur in any situation that a child has learned to associate with fear, shame, ridicule or vulnerability. Examples might include any form of public speaking, asking for help, trying something new and exposing themselves to the scrutiny of others or situations that risk potential failure.

To help your child overcome safety-related avoidance behaviour it is important to acknowledge that this behaviour has played an important role in your child's life so far. Safety behaviours have been your child's most important coping mechanism and survival tool.

It is helpful to reframe and normalize safety behaviour to your child; they might otherwise feel deeply ashamed of their feelings of vulnerability. Your child won't be able to relinquish this behaviour until they experience *both* physical and psychological safety. They will need to understand the important role these behaviours have played in their life and will also need the skills to manage feelings of terror, shame or vulnerability in another way.

The first step in addressing safety behaviours is to *normalize* feelings of shame and fear for children. Explain to your child how these behaviours are normal, understandable and clever survival skills for children who have felt afraid and vulnerable in the past. Educate your child about trauma, fear and avoidance and how clever children invent ways to keep themselves safe from overwhelmingly bad feelings. It is also helpful to provide them with the words to describe their feelings (see Chapter 6 for tips on how to build your child's emotional literacy and repertoire of feelings words). Create a family in which feelings are taken seriously and validated.

The second step is to understand your child's triggers and help them to build up their coping skills. Children who have experienced trauma can have a heightened level of arousal throughout the day. This means that it doesn't take as much to tip them into a fear and avoidance cycle as children who haven't experienced a lot of fear in their early lives. It will be helpful to teach them the skills to reduce their 'baseline' level of arousal, using coping skills like relaxation and mindfulness (the ability to be fully present in the moment). There a number of readily available apps and programs that you can practise with your child. All children (and adults) can benefit from practising mindfulness and relaxation skills. If you are able to incorporate relaxation, yoga or other mindful activities into family routines, you will be providing your whole family with self-regulation skills that can be called on throughout life. The resources section at the back of this book provides some websites and apps that can help you and your child to practise mindfulness and relaxation.

It will also be important to develop an understanding of what situations might trigger your child (for example, public scrutiny where there is risk of humiliation or failure, reminders of past trauma). These are the situations in which your child can start to practise their coping skills, starting with triggering situations they find less threatening and gradually progressing to more difficult situations. Children can be taught to use coping self-talk in situations that are difficult; they can practise coping self-talk ahead of time to use in anticipation of fearful situations; for example, 'I'm safe now... I can cope with this... I'll use my deep breathing.' Teach your child a signal to use to let you know when they are anxious or feeling bad. Make sure you acknowledge this signal and reward your child for using their coping skills.

When your child is afraid of something tangible, involve them in creating a plan to tackle this. Create a plan for gradually exposing them to a situation they avoid but in very small increments. The trick is to take very small steps in the right direction, at a pace and level of discomfort that your child can just manage with support. This gives them opportunities, in a slow and methodical way, to experience success in coping with feelings of fear in small, manageable doses so that they build a sense of competence. Sometimes you'll hear this referred to as a fear ladder or fear hierarchy.

Psychologists are skilled at helping you create and implement a systematic approach to overcoming your child's fears. If your child has powerful fear responses that appear to come 'out of the blue', this may mean they are remembering and re-experiencing a traumatic event and this re-living experience has been triggered by something (a sight, sound or sensation) that reminded them of a traumatic event. If this is a concern for your child, they will benefit from trauma processing therapy, delivered by a mental health professional.

Give your child confidence that they can learn to tackle their fears. At some level, they may have very little belief in their ability to cope with overwhelming emotions. This is because past trauma or humiliation at the hands of powerful others were associated with overwhelming hopelessness and powerlessness. Children who have experienced trauma can develop a 'learned helplessness': a deep belief that they can't control anything in their life; a sense of being at the mercy of others' whims. For this reason, it is important to help your child to distinguish between what they can and can't control. Let your child know that there are things they can do to manage and cope (that they do have some control over that aspect of their life). Expose your child to positive role models, including young adults who have overcome adversity. You can source a local support group, moderated internet support group, or talk to a local care-leavers group to find appropriate role models that have overcome adversity.

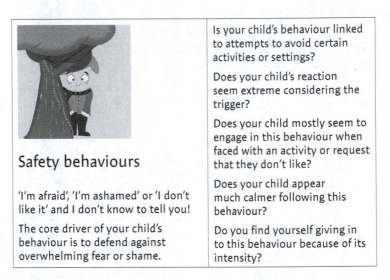

Safety behaviours	
'I'm afraid', 'I'm ashamed' or 'I don't like it' and I don't know to tell you!	Is your child's behaviour linked to attempts to avoid certain activities or settings?
	Does your child's reaction seem extreme considering the trigger?
	Does your child mostly seem to engage in this behaviour when faced with an activity or request that they don't like?
The core driver of your child's behaviour is to defend against overwhelming fear or shame.	Does your child appear much calmer following this behaviour?
	Do you find yourself giving in to this behaviour because of its intensity?

Boundary behaviours

A boundary behaviour is a behaviour that occurs when your child is trying to manage the availability and closeness of important people in their lives. Boundary behaviour is intimately tied to the unspoken and implicit beliefs about relationship that a child forms as a result of their early caregiving experience (we touched on these in Chapter 1 when we looked at how early adversity affects children's beliefs about relationships).

The hallmark feature of boundary behaviour is that it is normally only directed towards significant adults in the child's life. It's about managing their 'personal boundaries' and will occur when there has been some violation of their internalized belief about how a relationship should look – should it be rejecting and aloof? Should it be overly dependent and enmeshed? These behaviours are sometimes called 'attachment behaviours' because they are usually learnt in the context of your child's very early caregiving relationship. The child engages in this behaviour because at some level it makes them feel more protected and safe. By controlling the 'emotional proximity' of the important adults in their life, they feel a sense of control over the availability of important adults on whom they rely.

The core driver of your child's behaviour is to defend against overwhelming need and vulnerability.

The key messages your child is communicating to you through this behaviour are:

- I need you right now.

- I can't cope without you.

- I need space from you.

- I'm scared of feeling this close to you.

- I'm scared you will abandon me.

- And I don't know how else to tell you!

Boundary behaviours tend to be the most distressing and frustrating to foster and adoptive parents. They invoke feelings of rejection and often generate an anxiety that the child is 'damaged' in some way.

To better understand personal boundary behaviours we need to compare our experience of early life with that of a child in care. You and I are probably comfortable with affection and close, intimate relationships. The experience of relationship has been very different for some children.

For a child who has had difficult early relationships, it can feel very unsafe to rely on others. Children with adverse caregiving experiences can learn that needing comfort and support and asking for it in a straightforward way is not tolerated. They very quickly learn to use their behaviour to mask their genuine needs, and to signal their distress and need for comfort in different ways than you or I. Even very young children can learn that their need for intimacy and affection makes them vulnerable, and they develop a set of protective behaviours that help them feel like they can control their caregiver, who is their primary source of comfort at times of distress. These behaviours are ways to keep their caregiver close by, without angering them and therefore risking abandonment.

These kinds of 'boundary' behaviours are most perplexing to foster and adoptive carers as they often appear to arise suddenly and often when you are feeling close connection and enjoying your time together.

How do these kinds of behaviours come about? In a 'normal' early caregiving relationship a child learns very early on that their parent will respond reliably and calmly when they signal their distress. However, children with abusive or neglectful parents learn that the only way to guarantee their caregiver's attention is *not to signal their distress directly* and to behave in a way that is tolerated by the adult in their life.

A child whose parent is inconsistently attentive learns that the only way to ensure an adult is 'available' to them is to be overly dramatic and needy. They really need to 'turn up the volume' on their distress in order for it to get noticed. They learn that they need to be overly emotional – 'larger than life' – and dependent to keep their parent close by and responsive.

A child whose parent shuns or rejects them when they are in real emotional distress learns that the only way to ensure an adult is 'available' to them is to be self-sufficient. They learn that they need to 'shut down' their emotions to keep their parent close by and responsive.

In the latter two cases, when a child has experienced either inconsistent or unresponsive parenting, he/she learns that their authentic need for comfort will not be noticed and responded to in any reliable way. In both of these cases, a child learns to distort their feelings and comfort-seeking behaviour in order to placate an unpredictable or unresponsive parent. The child learns to 'signal' an adult in ways that their parent can tolerate, but which don't seem to make any sense to others.

- The core function of boundary behaviour is to manage the unpleasant vulnerability feelings that come with genuine need. For this reason it is powerfully reinforcing behaviour and can take some time to diminish.

- Boundary behaviour is any behaviour that serves to control your physical proximity or your emotional availability. It signals that your child is anxious and uncomfortable with your current emotional or physical proximity (they feel you are too emotionally distant or too close).

- Boundary behaviour means that your child, because of powerful early learning experiences, lacks trust and confidence that you will be consistently emotionally and physically available, just because they need and deserve this. At a deep level, they feel they need to control you through their behaviour (and thereby ensure you stay nearby) by engaging in dramatic, dependent and attention-seeking behaviour on the one hand, or distancing and rejecting behaviour on the other hand.

Each child's boundary behaviour will look different, and it depends on whether they feel most comfortable being self-reliant and rejecting, or dependent, demanding and needy. Remember your child's behaviour is based on powerful early learning that has taught them that this behaviour is the only way to control important adults in their life.

Each type of boundary behaviour (demanding or distancing) is triggered by different things:

- *Demanding behaviours:* Dependent, demanding and dramatic behaviour is triggered by an underlying anxiety that you are not emotionally 'available' and can't be relied on to respond when needed. These kinds of boundary behaviours serve to keep you close and ensure you attend to their needs on their terms. These behaviours send you the message that your child can't cope without you. Through this behaviour, your child is able to gain a sense of control over you to ensure you are always at hand when needed, and on their terms. In this way, they re-establish a boundary that they feel comfortable with and that matches their unspoken belief about what the parent–child relationship should look like.

In managing this kind of behaviour, your aim is to gradually help your child to tolerate increasing periods of independence, without resorting to tantrums, violence or attention-seeking behaviour to ensure your availability. Teach your child the language and non-verbal means to signal they need you without resorting to challenging behaviours.

- *Distancing behaviours:* Distancing and rejecting behaviour is triggered by the feeling that you are too close (either emotionally or physically). Distancing behaviour usually follows a period of calm, comfortable and close interaction with you. These behaviours serve to 'push away' – to give you the message that they don't need you – and to re-create the feeling of autonomy, self-reliance and independence that they learned to rely on early in life. In this way, your child is able to re-establish a boundary that they feel comfortable with and that matches their unspoken belief about what the parent–child relationship should look like.

  In managing this kind of boundary behaviour, your aim is to gradually help your child to tolerate increasing periods of 'closeness' without resorting to distancing and rejecting behaviour. This will take time and you should expect to experience set-backs at times of stress, or when your child is tired or unwell. Teach your child the language or non-verbal means to signal that they need some time alone.

Over time, you will get to understand your child's triggers and the conditions under which this behaviour is more likely. Acknowledge and validate your child's discomfort when their relationship boundaries are crossed. Let them know that you understand how frightening it must be to feel that adults cannot be relied on. Provide your child with a means to signal when they need you or need space. Notice when your overly self-reliant child asks for you when distressed. Notice when your dependent child shows signs of independence and coping.

Remember that although these behaviours are frustrating and demoralizing, they are actually signals that you are important to them and they need you. It's not personal, even though you may be the person at the receiving end. Over time, these behaviours towards you are likely to diminish as a result of experiencing the care of a reliable and consistent caregiver.

　**Boundary behaviours**　'I need space' or 'I need you right now' and 'I don't know how to tell you!'　The core driver of your child's behaviour is to defend against overwhelming need and vulnerability.	Does your child mostly seem to engage in this behaviour when you and they are feeling close and sharing special time?　Does your child mostly seem to engage in this behaviour when you are preoccupied or feeling unwell?　Does your child react in overly dramatic ways to minor frustrations?　Does your child 'sabotage' activities you are enjoying together?　Does this behaviour only occur around the important adults in your child's life?

Self-regulation behaviours

A regulation behaviour is any behaviour that your child engages in when they are feeling overwhelmed or overstimulated and are trying to calm and regulate their arousal level. This kind of behaviour is common amongst children who are more sensitive to their sensory environment (children with sensory regulation difficulties), who are more sensitive to their internal sensations (thirst, hunger) or who are more easily overwhelmed by their emotions. Self-regulation behaviours are common amongst children with autism or FASD. These kinds of behaviours also appear common amongst children who have been exposed to early life adversity and have difficulty managing strong emotions (see Chapter 6), or difficulty in sensory regulation (see Chapter 4). They may also be more common when your child is hungry, tired, thirsty or sick. The core driver of your child's behaviour is to defend against overwhelming feelings of dys-regulation and dis-ease.

The key messages your child is communicating to you through this behaviour are:

- I'm overwhelmed.

- I'm dys-regulated.

- I can't bring myself back to calm.

- And I don't know how else to tell you!

In order to manage this kind of behaviour it is important to understand how your child experiences the world and their internal sensations and feelings (hunger, thirst or strong emotions). The first step is making the connection between external and internal triggers and your child's behaviour.

Managing 'external' triggers

Support your child to develop an awareness of what aspects of their surroundings 'wind them up' and what aspects of the sensory world they find calming (see Chapter 4). Consider how you can modify the sensory environment to better suit your child. Develop and practise sensory regulation skills that your child can use in different settings (this is discussed more in Chapter 4).

MANAGING 'INTERNAL' TRIGGERS

Children with this kind of difficulty also benefit from strategies to predict and regulate their internal world. Some children do not accurately recognize and respond to their internal bodily sensations. Internal bodily sensations like feelings of hunger, tiredness, thirst or emotional states may not properly 'register' in the same way that we are able to recognize these internal sensations.

Emotions can be difficult for children to identify and control. Many children are easily overwhelmed by emotions that they cannot name or regulate by themselves. A common example of this occurs in the lead up to, and aftermath of, a child's contact with their biological family. These children benefit from developing a feelings vocabulary and from 'touching base' or 'grounding' activities on the lead up to, and aftermath of, emotionally charged events (more information on this is available in Chapter 6).

Bodily sensations can also be hard for children to recognize. Many adopted and fostered children have difficulty in discriminating between bodily sensations such as hunger and emotions such as anger; they frequently 'misrecognize' hunger as anger, or vice versa. This means they will present as angry when they are in fact hungry but lack the ability to recognize this. This may sound strange; however, little children rely on a responsive caregiver to help them learn to name internal sensations like hunger, thirst and feelings.

Instead, all internal sensations are experienced as a similar sense of 'dis-ease' – feeling uneasy and unregulated – without being able to name what it is they need. These children will benefit from going 'back to basics'; you will need to help them to accurately identify and name what messages their body is sending them (to discriminate what hunger, thirst and fatigue feel like in their bodies and to recognize what emotions feel like in their bodies).

Self-regulation behaviours

'I'm overwhelmed', 'I'm dys-regulated', 'I don't know how to bring myself back to calm' and 'I don't know how to tell you'.

The core driver of your child's behaviour is to defend against overwhelming dy-sregulation and dis-ease.

Does your child mostly seem to engage in this behaviour when tired or unwell?

Does your child's behaviour seem linked to certain sensory stimuli or settings?

Does your child appear much calmer after engaging in this behaviour?

Do you find yourself avoiding certain activities or settings because you know that they will affect your child's behaviour?

Is this behaviour more likely following emotional activities (e.g. visiting biological family)?

Skills deficit behaviours

These behaviours occur when your child becomes frustrated by demands that exceed their current ability and skills. This could be due to intellectual delay, delayed social skills, poor organization and planning, poor memory, or language and communication problems. Delays in any of these skills – skills that are central to socially competent behaviour – are likely to cause avoidance, frustration and non-compliance.

The core driver of your child's behaviour is to defend against overwhelming difficulty in coping with your expectations.

The key messages your child is communicating to you through this behaviour are:

- I can't do it.

- I can't understand.

- I don't feel safe letting you know I can't do it.

- And I don't know how else to tell you!

In general, the more areas of developmental delay your child is experiencing, the more likely this kind of behaviour is to emerge. It reflects a 'mismatch' between our behavioural expectations of the child and what they are currently capable of. This mismatch, if undetected, leads to feelings of frustration and inadequacy which the child communicates through their behaviour.

In general, the more areas of developmental delay your child is experiencing, the more you will need to accommodate their needs and modify your expectations of them.

- Skills deficit behaviours are about the child lacking the skills to do what you're asking of them. These are the difficulties associated with developmental difference and delays in the key cognitive skills required to keep pace with our social and learning environment.

- Skills deficit behaviours are more likely in unstructured situations in which expectations become unclear and may be more likely in children with diagnoses such as autism, FASD and ADHD.

- Skills deficit behaviours are improved by modifying or clarifying expectations, simplifying interactions, providing structure and predictability and teaching the necessary skills.

Children with this kind of difficulty will benefit from maintaining a highly structured environment in which expectations are made clear. The greater the deficit, the more you will need to modify the environment to suit your child. I call this 'scaffolding' the child's development. Just like scaffolding is used to prop up a building until it is completed, you provide the necessary scaffolding to support your child until such time as they have the skills they need to succeed.

In each of the remaining chapters in this book, we'll look at how to modify the environment to better suit your child. Simple ways to scaffold and simplify the environment include enhancing structure and predictability, using visual prompts and pacing tasks and instructions.

Children with this kind of difficulty will also need your support to build skills that are missing. It is easier to do this if you have a good understanding of your child's developmental level. Set your expectations at your child's *current developmental level*, not their current *chronological age*. Focus on one skill at a time, based on their current skills and functioning, and aim to build up their competence and skill over time.

Skill deficits behaviours 'I can't do it' or 'I can't understand' and 'I don't know how to tell you!' The core driver of your child's behaviour is to defend against overwhelming difficulty in coping with expectations.	Does your child mostly seem to engage in this behaviour when faced with unstructured or unpredictable settings? Does your child seem to struggle to understand what you are asking? Does your child express this behaviour when faced with difficult tasks? Does your child manage better in highly structured settings? Has your child been assessed as having delayed development in any area (speech, cognitive, motor (physical), reading, spelling or maths)?

In the remainder of this book, we'll look in more detail at the kinds of skill deficits that we believe are common amongst children who have experienced early adversity; these are their *developmental differences* in the areas of sensory processing, language and cognitive skills. As we'll see, supporting the child with developmental difference will *always* involve a combination of the following:

- Modifying your expectations of your child – re-setting expectations to meet their current abilities. Remind yourself, it's not that your child *won't*, it's that they *can't*.

- Modifying the environment to enable your child to be successful (simplifying, using visual prompts and modifying how you give instructions to children).

- Supporting your child to develop social and behavioural competence, by teaching them missing coping skills.

For more detail about the behaviours covered in this chapter and how to support your child visit the Fostering Difference website.

Chapter 4

Developmental Difference in Sensory Regulation

In this chapter, we'll look at one of the key reasons why children have difficulty with self-regulation and behaviour: namely their altered sensitivity to the sensory environment. This developmental difference is common amongst children with FASD or autism, but we believe it is also common amongst children who have experienced early adversity. First, let's explore what is meant by sensory regulation difficulties.

Normal and impaired sensory processing

Most of us don't notice the way that our external world is constantly bombarding us with sensory information. At the same time, we are constantly receiving sensory feedback about what our bodies are doing, and how our bodies are positioned in space. At any point in time masses of incoming sensory information is simultaneously collected and processed by our brains. This is typically done without any conscious effort on our part, and this smooth and effortless processing is something we very much take for granted.

Most of us are able to trust our sensory and bodily information; our brain and our senses work seamlessly together to process multiple and competing sensory inputs at any one time and to give us a reliable picture of what is happening in the world. For children with sensory processing disorder, however, this process is far from effortless or seamless.

Let's take an example to explain what a sensory processing disorder might feel like. As you read this book, your senses are working together automatically, and mostly outside of your conscious awareness, to help you process what you are reading. At the same time that you are reading this, you may be aware of background noise, of sensations like a dry mouth, the sensation of your clothes on your body, and the feel of your body on your chair. All of this sensory information is processed effortlessly by your brain, and at the same time. Because you do not have a sensory processing difficulty, you are able to automatically filter out the unnecessary sensory information in order to pay full attention to the words on this page. Because you don't have difficulty with sensory integration and regulation, this process in effortless and automatic, and you are well able to stay alert and focused enough to keep reading this book.

This experience is very different for a child with sensory processing difficulties. A child with this developmental difference may find it impossible to concentrate on reading a book. This child might be aware of the scratching from their clothes, the noises in the background, the feel of their body in the chair, the buzz of the fluorescent light above them. Because they can't automatically screen out all this competing sensory information, their brain easily becomes overwhelmed and they would have difficulty concentrating and remaining alert.

Sensory processing difficulties also affect a child's level of arousal in a sensory rich environment. This difficulty affects a child's capacity to maintain optimal levels of arousal and alertness. It can make them sleepy and under-alert, or it can make them hyperactive and over-stimulated.

While your child can't control their sensory sensitivities and how they respond to the sensory world, they can develop an understanding of their own unique sensory profile and therefore understand how to better manage their sensory environment. Your child might otherwise have difficulty in maintaining concentration and alertness in situations where sustained focus is needed (e.g. the classroom). We can really help a child by supporting them to develop an understanding of how they respond to the sensory world and to develop the skills to accommodate their sensory 'skin'. The world can be an exhausting and overstimulating place for a child with sensory processing difficulties unless they know how to manage it.

Your child's sensory processing isn't within their conscious control; it's not a choice, it's an automatic bodily function.

So how do you know whether or not your child has difficulty in processing and integrating the sensory world? Your child's sensory processing difference can take many different forms. A child with sensory issues may under-respond or over-respond to sensory input, leading them to avoid or seek out different sensory experiences. Your child may have difficulty in integrating and distinguishing between relevant and competing sensory input, leading to fatigue and avoidance of stressful sensory environments. If your child has this kind of developmental difference:

- Your child might show over-sensitivity to one or more sensory forms (e.g. touch, light or sound), leading to avoidance or panic reactions when they cannot avoid these overwhelming sensations.

- Your child might under-react to sensory stimulation. In this case they will seek out extreme or intense sensory experiences.

- Your child's sensory sensitivities might result in highly unusual levels of physical activity (meaning your child's energy levels will be either too high or they'll become under-active).

- Your child's sensory sensitivities might result in fluctuating levels of alertness and arousal. Too much time spent trying to concentrate in a classroom, for example, or too much noise, might affect your child's level of alertness – make your child sleepy or hyperactive – if they are not able to use sensory regulation strategies to keep themselves at an optimal level of arousal.

- Your child's difficulty with sensory processing and processing feedback from bodily sensations (proprioception) might mean that your child is clumsy and has difficulty with coordination.

- Your child's inefficiency in sensory processing might mean that they fatigue easily when engaging any one sensory modality for prolonged periods (e.g. listening) without enlisting competing sensory input (fidgeting, scribbling or sucking on a lolly).

- Your child might have difficulty in filtering out irrelevant sensory information. When there is lots of sensory information coming in simultaneously, they cannot filter out distracting sensory information, leading to sensory overload.

We don't really seem to have a good understanding of how early adversity is linked to sensory processing difficulties. We believe that the difficulty lies in the brain's automatic processing of sensory information and how efficiently this occurs. This means that children *cannot control* how sensory information is processed by their brains. We can think of sensory processing as more like an automatic bodily function (like our heart beat or our digestion) – it's not something we can consciously control. Affected children are frequently exhausted by school in particular, because of the need to process a super-sensory environment while maintaining the 'calm and alert' state needed for optimal learning.

In this chapter, we look at some basic principles for understanding and responding to your child's sensory skin. The area of sensory processing and sensory integration disorders is complex, and can involve problems with balance and posture, or body awareness or body coordination as well, since these rely on sensory input to work efficiently. Sensory processing and modulation difficulties occur:

- When your child cannot properly process information coming in from the senses (taste, touch, smell, sight, sound).

- When your child has difficulty in filtering out sensory distractions. They cannot filter out unessential sensory information, causing sensory overload. The more senses that are being stimulated, the worse this situation is for children.

- When your child's central nervous system does not respond normally to sensory stimulation – either over- or under-reacting to normal sensory stimulation (e.g. being touched).

- When your child struggles if required to sustain focus in situations in which multiple sensory input information has to be integrated (e.g. the classroom), causing difficult behaviour aimed at helping them cope with being overwhelmed.

The following are some of the most commonly reported, and easily observed, issues in children with sensory issues:

- Avoidance of certain situations or sensations. Over-sensitivity to one (or more) sensory form (e.g. touch, movement or sounds). This can lead to avoidance of textures, touch, sounds, etc. The child can panic or have an extreme behavioural reaction if they are unable to avoid these overwhelming sensations.

- Seeking out certain situations or sensations due to under-reacting to sensory stimulation. In this case, the child seems to seek out extreme or intense sensory experiences, like loud noises, crashing into objects, whirling and spinning.

- Unusual levels of physical activity (either extremely high or low). This also occurs with difficulty in executive functioning and other childhood difficulties such as ADHD.

- Fluctuating levels of alertness. The child's arousal level changes in response to the sensory environment (e.g. too much time spent listening in a classroom environment; too much visual stimulation/bright lights). The child can become quite sleepy or hyperactive in certain settings.

- Trouble with coordination. In this case a child can be clumsy and have difficulty in learning new behaviours and tasks involving motor coordination due to poor sensory feedback from their bodies.

This is a rapidly developing field, and a complete coverage of the range of difficulties linked to sensory processing is beyond the scope of this book. This chapter will focus on common issues that affect a child's attention and readiness for learning and on the sensory triggers that cause explosive behaviour and meltdowns due to overstimulation.

If, after reading this chapter, you would like a more comprehensive understanding of your child's sensory profile, I recommend discussing your child's needs with a children's occupational therapist. Children with ASD and FASD are likely to experience extreme sensitivity to their sensory environment and children with these diagnoses will benefit from the specialized support of an occupational therapist.

Principles for supporting a child's sensory processing

Let's look at the basic steps to supporting a child with sensory sensitivities next. In starting to think about your child's sensory sensitivities, you might find it helpful to use one of the many sensory checklists included in the resources section at the end of this book. You can use checklists as a starting point to developing an individualized response to your child's needs.

In understanding and managing your child's sensory differences it can be useful to follow these steps:

Step one: observe your child across a range of settings to determine their main sensory style

The first step in understanding your child's 'sensory skin' is to put aside some time to observe your child and how they are affected by the environment. Ask yourself: 'How does the sensory environment "trigger" my child?'; 'What aspects of the sensory world does my child like or avoid?' It is also important to observe whether and how the sensory environment affects your child's arousal level: 'In which sensory environments does my child start to get sleepy/wound up?' Finally, consider how your child's attention and concentration is affected by their sensory issues and what might help them to concentrate for more extended periods of time: 'What situations make it hard for my child to sit still and concentrate?'; and 'What does this tell me about how to make the world more manageable for my child?' You will usually notice that your child's sensory style will take a pattern. Here are some clues to your child's sensory style.

For example, if your child *over-reacts* to sensory stimulation, you may find the following:

- Your child doesn't like being touched, especially light touch. They will seem to reject your physical affection and hugs.

- Your child is bothered by certain textures of clothing fabric, is irritated by clothing tags and avoids touching certain textures.

- Your child is bothered by bright lights or certain patterns and blinks or squints often. These children may find the dark calming and may fatigue easily if working on bright computer screens.

- Your child is sensitive to sounds and background noise. They may find everyday noises overwhelming, or just too loud to manage. They may often hold their hands over their ears as an attempt to block out the noise

- Your child doesn't like certain tastes or is extremely fussy about the texture or temperature of food. They may avoid any food with strong tastes or textures.

- Your child may resist brushing their teeth, avoid being touched on the face or having their face washed. Your child can become distressed or angry when their hair is touched/shampooed or cut.

- Your child may recoil at many everyday smells; they may form a strong like or dislike of a person, based on their smell.

Children with this developmental difference can display challenging behaviour that is linked to avoiding sensations that they find strongly aversive.

If your child *under-responds* to the sensory world, you may find the following:

- Your child needs to touch everything (e.g. they always touch doorframes when passing through; they touch walls when walking past).

- Your child seeks out movements that give strong sensory feedback (e.g. they may lie with their head upside down on the couch; they may need to put everything in their mouth, for example chewing on clothing or jewellery).

- Your child may feel compelled to touch textures and surfaces that provide a comforting experience (e.g. favourite blanket).

- Your child may have difficulty in holding and using tools that rely on sensory feedback from the body (e.g. scissors, pens, forks).

- Your child may have difficulty in orienting and coordinating their body to get dressed; you may find that they are a sloppy dresser or appear messy.

- Your child may have difficulty in registering their sensory environment and in using sensory stimulations like morning light to get going in the morning. They might seem lazy and unmotivated.

- Your child can have difficulty in noticing if their hands or face are dirty.

- Your child may not notice when they have injured themselves.

- Your child constantly fiddles with anything within reach and needs to touch everything.

- Your child constantly chews on pens and pencils and prefers food with very strong tastes. They may seek out a food or drink based on its ability to provide sensory input (e.g. sour or salty foods, crunchy foods or extremely hot or cold foods).

- Your child prefers to sleep under heavy blankets and seeks out 'squishing' sensations.

- Your child needs to smell everything, shows preference for strong smells, but may be unable to detect bad food by smell.

- Your child seeks out 'rough play', enjoys tackling and wrestling games and is often bumping into other children.

- Your child may prefer bright colours.

- Your child may talk louder than necessary and have difficulty modulating their voice to match the speaker and the situation.

Children with this developmental difference can display challenging behaviour that is linked to seeking out physical contact and constantly fidgeting with objects in settings where this is not allowed.

If your child has difficulty in *processing the sensory information* that is coming in from their bodily sensations – for example, sensory information about the position of their bodies in space or about the internal sensations of their bodies (e.g. hunger) – you might notice the following behavioural clues:

- Your child may have problems in realizing where their body is in space or in coordinating their bodies in space, meaning they bump into objects frequently.

- Your child may have difficulty in judging how much pressure to apply when picking up objects, often resulting in objects getting broken. They may play with others too roughly, hurting them.

- Your child might have difficulty in discriminating tactile sensations and may react equally badly to a cut or the feel of the shower on their skin.

- Your child might avoid activities that move the body in certain ways (e.g. that involve balance, hand–eye coordination, climbing or lifting their feet off the ground).

- Your child might seem clumsy, have poor body awareness and frequently knock things over.

- Your child may have difficulty in 'noticing' internal bodily sensations; they may not notice when hungry or need reminding to eat or drink.

These are some of the common difficulties you might notice. Your child can show a mixture of any, or all, of the difficulties listed above. For example, your child might over-react to some sensory stimuli (e.g. noise) but under-react to others (e.g. touch). Each child's sensory style will be unique to them and the relationship between your child's sensory sensitivities and their behaviour will also be unique to them. Your child's sensory preferences may also be affected by a history of past trauma, and it is important to consider this when thinking about developing coping and soothing strategies for your child (see Box 5).

BOX 5

The impact of trauma on the selection of sensory regulation strategies

It is critically important to consider the impact of trauma before you start to address a child's sensory difficulties. This is important because childhood trauma can cause many symptoms that are similar to sensory processing disorder and it is very important to be aware of your child's traumatic past when considering which strategies might help them. This is most obvious when it comes to how a child reacts to touch in all forms.

For example, a child who recoils from touch can do this because of sensory sensitivity but this kind of aversion can be trauma related for children that have learned to associate touch from an adult with a painful or traumatic memory. Perhaps touch has been associated with sexual abuse in the past. In this case, you will need to be extremely cautious in using any strategies that involve physical touch or restriction of movement.

Similarly, a child can avoid body movement because of their trauma history, rather than having sensory issues. A child who has difficulty in controlling and coordinating their body in space may avoid exercise because it is an unpleasant sensory experience. However, aversion to exercise can also be related to a past trauma. A traumatized child can come to associate benign sensations such as their rapidly beating heart with past trauma (it reminds them how their heart beat rapidly during a past frightening abuse). They avoid exercise because they want to avoid feeling as though they are re-living a past trauma. Therefore we need to be cautious in using body movement exercises as a form of sensory regulation (e.g. star jumps or running upstairs).

Step two: compile a profile of your child's sensory likes and dislikes

Once you have begun observing your child, it can be helpful to sit down with them and complete a sensory calming chart. To start with, this should be done by simply identifying their sensory likes and dislikes. I've included an example of a calming chart with some example activities here. What calms your child will be completely different from what calms another child. I've also included a chart for recording what kinds of sensory inputs cause your child stress. Once again, each child will be triggered by different things in their sensory world. The charts you end up with will be unique to your child and based on their unique sensory needs. I've included blank charts in the Appendices at the end of this book that you can photocopy and update as you learn more about your child's needs.

MY SENSORY 'LIKES'	
THESE THINGS HELP ME STAY CALM	
	SIGHT Keep the lighting dim
	TOUCH Use deep pressure (pillow 'sandwich') Use weighted blanket at bedtime
	HEARING Keep headphones on when on computer to screen out background noise
	SMELL Lemons Lavender oil
	TASTE Suck on a sour lolly Drink icy cold water

Source: Adapted from Fostering Difference www.fosteringdifference.com.au

MY SENSORY 'DISLIKES' THESE THINGS STRESS ME OUT	
SIGHT Bright lights Computer screens Fluorescent lights	
TOUCH Unexpected touch Light touch	
HEARING Background noise, especially voices	
SMELL e.g. compost	
TASTE Squishy textures Mixing textures together	

Source: Adapted from Fostering Difference www.fosteringdifference.com.au

Step three: build sensory regulation activities into your child's day

The next thing to consider is how to build sensory calming strategies into their everyday life and activities. Your aim is to help them to build up a repertoire of sensory coping 'habits' that they can incorporate into their daily routine. At first, they will need your support with this.

The trick is to use your child's reactivity to the sensory world as a means to calm them, rather than 'wind them up'. Just as your child's sensory sensitivity causes them to become dys-regulated (when the sensory world is working against them) you can also use their reactivity to the sensory world to calm them too (when you let the sensory world work for them).

Start by taking the sensory activities listed in their sensory calming chart (using the blank sensory likes and dislikes charts found in Appendix A and B). Your child's sensory likes can be used to calm them. Your child's sensory dislikes should be avoided as much as possible. This is the simplest way to start building a sensory regulation strategy that works for your child. Start by embedding sensory coping strategies into one aspect of your child's day and then build up to using them at regular intervals throughout their day.

Once you have a good idea of your child's sensory likes and dislikes, you can start looking at more sophisticated approaches that are effective in helping your child to concentrate for extended periods of time without becoming hyperactive or sleepy.

These strategies involve body and muscle works as well as these are much more effective in helping your child to achieve optimal levels of alertness and readiness to learn. They can also involve engaging 'competing' senses to assist in your child's concentration when required to sit still. So we can use all five of your child's senses and also their body work as ways to regulate. It's ideal to develop strategies that can be used in a range of settings as well as strategies that can be used throughout the day. These strategies can form a sensory regulation plan that can help your child to concentrate in a range of learning environments. On page 80 there is an example of what a completed sensory regulation plan might look like (there is also a blank template for you to use in Appendix C at the end of this book). For now, let's look at ways to develop a more complex sensory regulation plan to help your child to concentrate in learning environments.

There are two main ways to build regulation strategies that are useful in maintaining children's concentration and attention:

1. by regularly building in sensory strategies throughout your child's day to help them regulate

2. by engaging competing senses to assist concentration.

Let's look at some examples.

ENGAGING SENSORY STRATEGIES AT REGULAR INTERVALS TO HELP THEM REGULATE

There are a range of different activities that can be enlisted to help the child who has sensory dysregulation. Use these kinds of activities at regular intervals throughout the day to keep your child regulated and calm and to maintain optimal concentration and attention. These regulation activities can involve whole body movements that engage the larger, deep muscle groups; using touch strategies that calm and using taste senses in 'mouth work'. Here are some examples:

- *Whole body movement strategies:* Involve your child in regular movement of the whole body – think 'soothe as you move'. Example activities include bouncing on a trampoline or mini-trampoline, doing star jumps or whole body squats, spinning on a giant swing or rubber tyre or running up a set of stairs. Do these activities at regular intervals or between classes to help your child to concentrate.

- *Large muscle work:* Have your child do regular seated chair 'push-ups' between class activities (in which they lift their own weight off the chair while seated); get your child to do push-pull activities (e.g. lift up chairs and place on desk; mop the floor; push against the wall) or involve your child in lifting heavy objects (for example, ask them to carry in the shopping or to carry piles of books for the teacher between classes).

- *Touch strategies:* Examples of touch strategies that can be used to calm your child throughout the day include applying deep pressure (tight bear hugs); using weighted blankets; giving your child a 'pillow sandwich' between two large cushions or letting them sit holding a heat pack (*but* check with your child first before using touch).

- *Mouth work:* Involve your child in working their mouth against resistance. Try asking them to suck through a long twisted straw (drinking against resistance). Allow your child to suck on a sour lolly, crunch on their favourite crunchy food (e.g. celery) or you may be able to give them crushed ice or ice cubes to suck on. Any activity that involves your child in working their mouth against resistance and meets their sensory needs will help them to stay regulated throughout the day.

Once you know what works for your child, you should aim to incorporate these strategies into regular intervals in your child's day (for example, ask them to do five squats between activities).

ENGAGING YOUR CHILD'S COMPETING SENSES TO HELP THEM CONCENTRATE

Engage your child's 'competing' senses in any activity that requires attention, concentration and fine motor coordination. This means making sure your child's other senses are engaged when they need to sit still and concentrate (for example, when doing schoolwork or completing any writing task). Teachers are becoming more aware of the need to use these sensory strategies to assist children with sensory sensitivities to be successful in the classroom environment. Here are some examples:

- *Engage 'competing' senses:* Engaging a different sense can help prevent any one of your child's senses from becoming overloaded. For example, playing music through headphones may help your child focus on writing. In class, a child can suck on a chewy necklace, or a sour or chewy lolly to help them to concentrate on what the teacher is saying. Using fidgets, or allowing them to use squeeze toys or doodle on paper can help them to listen for extended periods of time. Allowing them to engage large muscle groups (for example, by letting them do seated push-ups in their chair) can also help the child to concentrate for extended periods of time.

- *Engage fine motor feedback:* When your child needs to sit and listen allow them to use rubber fidgets and quiet squeeze toys. Let them doodle with pen and paper – all these strategies help concentration and listening in class.

- *Engage big muscles:* Engaging your child's large, deep muscle groups in resistance work provides a sense of deep pressure that helps them maintain optimal arousal. Build regular big muscle group strategies into breaks between classroom activities. For example, your child's teacher could ask them to take down chairs from the desks at the start of the day, ask them to do seated push-ups in their chair, ask them to move a weighted chair between activities or to carry piles of books between classes. At home, you can build in regular 'muscle break' activities like pushing against the wall or moving a weighted chair; or create mini swinging, bouncing or running breaks.

COMPILE A SENSORY PLAN FOR CONCENTRATION

You may find it useful to complete a sensory plan that lists the activities your child can do before or during schoolwork. I've included an example of what this might look like when completed (see 'My sensory plan: these things help me stay focused'). An occupational therapist can also assist with a range of strategies that will make fine motor tasks less fatiguing for your child. Of course, it will be essential to involve your child's teacher in any plans that involve sensory techniques being used in the classroom. You will also find a blank sensory plan chart at the end of this book that you can photocopy and discuss with the relevant professional.

MY SENSORY PLAN

THESE THINGS HELP ME STAY FOCUSED

	SIGHT Sit up the front of the class to avoid visual distractions
	TOUCH Use fidget toys when listening to the teacher
	HEARING Block out voices with white noise
	SMELL Use my scented handkerchief to smell
	TASTE Use my chew necklace Suck against resistance using a long straw Suck on a sour lolly at break times
	MOVING MY BODY Walk up and down a nearby flight of stairs
	USING BIG MUSCLES Do five seated push-ups before listening to story time

Source: Adapted from Fostering Difference www.fosteringdifference.com.au

Remember that traumatized children can have strong negative reactions to touch or to certain body positions. It is really important to check that you have the child's permission to try *any* sensory calming technique in case it brings back memories of trauma. This doesn't mean you can't use sensory strategies, just that you might have to adapt these to suit your child. For example, they may not be able to tolerate calming muscle pressure in the form of bear hugs but the same kind of pressure from a weighted blanket could be comforting. It's always important to consider how a regulation strategy could affect your child. Check out your ideas with the child before using them.

Step four: practise, review and revise

Once you have developed an understanding of your child's sensory sensitivities, and preferred calming and regulating strategies, it is time to try out strategies with your child. Start with situations in which their sensory issues affect their ability to participate in school or other activities. If you feel unsure, it's OK to start with a part of your child's daily routine instead. For example, you might start with strategies to help them to concentrate during homework time.

Prioritize 'transportable' skills wherever possible. By this I mean strategies your child can use in many different settings. For example, if your child finds smell calming, a handkerchief with essential oils on it might be a transportable strategy that could work for them. A fidget ball is an example of a transportable strategy that a child can use in a range of settings in which they need to concentrate for extended periods of time. Sour candy is another example that a child can use to regulate themselves across a range of settings.

It will also be very important to communicate what you have learned about your child's sensitivities and regulation needs to the other significant adults in their life. Your child's teacher will need to understand their sensory needs and agree to them using certain sensory strategies in the classroom. If they are unsure about this, you can suggest a trial – that it might be limited to certain classroom activities to start with. Good communication about your child's needs will help them to embed sensory coping strategies in all areas of their life. Remember your aim is to support your child to have their very best calm and alert day, wherever that may be.

Chapter 5

Developmental Difference in Language and Communication

In this chapter, we'll look at one of the key reasons why children have difficulty with behaviour: namely delays and difficulty with language and communication. This developmental difference is common amongst children with FASD or autism, but we believe it is also common amongst children who have experienced a range of early adversities. First, let's explore what is meant by language and communication difficulties.

What are language and communication difficulties?

Whether we realize it or not, we all rely on our language skills to help us to make sense of the world. Children who have difficulty in communicating or have difficulty in understanding what people say will find the social world confusing and frustrating.

Let's return to the example we used earlier in the book to explain. Imagine again that you have been magically transported to another country, in which everyone speaks a different language. How would you feel about the fact that everyone is speaking a language that you don't understand? How easy would it be for you to make yourself understood in this country? Perhaps, because you are clever, you can make people understand a few of your needs by using signing, gestures or pictures. On the whole, though, I guess you'd feel pretty lonely. You'd have no way of letting people know your thoughts or feelings. You'd have no way of communicating your hopes or dreams.

The child who has language and communication difficulties will often have the feeling that others are 'speaking a foreign language'. A child with this developmental difference will have difficulty in making themselves understood and in connecting with others on an emotional level. Is it any wonder that a child with this developmental difference is so often frustrated and angry? Is it surprising that they lash out, or pretend to understand when they don't?

Children in adoptive or foster care often have *delayed* or *disordered* language and communication skills. (We'll talk more about the difference between language delay and language disorder later in this chapter.) These difficulties often go undetected and unsupported, for a range of reasons. As we'll see, some forms of language difficulty aren't easy to pick up while others are more obvious. This chapter will explain some of the common language and communication problems and explain how you might recognize these. It will also include some strategies for supporting your child's language development where this is an issue.

Why worry about this form of developmental difference?

Language plays a very important role in children's social and emotional development. Socially skilled children rely on their language skills to express their feelings, to enquire about others' feelings, to express their needs and to advocate for others' needs. Language is central to logical and abstract thinking and self-reflection. Language skills play an important role in being able to predict consequences of actions and in engaging in coping self-talk – these are the foundation skills for developing behavioural self-control.

We know that there is a strong relationship between language difficulties and behaviour problems in children. A high proportion of children referred to a child mental health clinic for behaviour problems also have some language difficulty. Around half of all children who are assessed as having a language problem also show challenging and disruptive behaviour. In short, the relationship between language and communication difficulties and challenging social behaviour is robust although we don't fully understand why.

What's the relationship between early adversity and language difficulties?

Like many other aspects of children's development, children's language development occurs in the context of their social and caregiving relationships. Children are introduced to language through their early primary caregiving relationship. Through social interaction with their caregiver, and with their wider social network, they learn that language helps them to meet their needs.

Language develops in an interactive way; it is shaped from the very early interactions between a caregiver and their child that involve rhythmic sounds, and evolves into the sounds that we recognize as fully formed language and speech. Children learn that language is a powerful tool that helps them to convey their needs to their caregiver.

Language is complex. Everyday language is actually made up of a set of related skills that must all work smoothly together in order for someone to be a skilled communicator. A child needs to be able to listen, to understand, to form words and speak them clearly and in the correct order, and to communicate in a way that is matched to context. If any one of these complex and interrelated skills is missing, a child may have difficulty in using language to meet their needs in a social world. I'll talk a little more about how to support these language skills in this chapter.

Children's language can be affected by a range of factors. Certain medical conditions can affect speech and language development (such as epilepsy or Down's syndrome). Pregnancy and early childhood conditions that affect hearing can cause delays in speech and language development (such as repeated or untreated ear infections).

Family factors also play a role in language development. A family history of speech and language problems, a child's birth order, a child's gender, whether English is a first language and family discipline styles are all factors that have been associated with speech and language difficulties.

Exposure to early adversity also has a major impact on children's developing language skills. It does this in two main ways:

Speech and language delay

First, a child exposed to early adversity can experience *delayed development* of their speech and language. Delayed language development occurs when a child falls behind in their language development, when compared with other children of the same age. An example of this might be when a seven-year-old child is talking like a pre-schooler or doesn't yet know the name of the basic colours. If a child has speech or language delay, they are falling behind in one or more areas of speech and language development. For example, they may have difficulty with spoken language, they may have difficulty in understanding and reproducing the individual sounds that make up words, or they may struggle with naming objects that other children of the same age can name easily.

A child who has a speech or language delay might otherwise be following a relatively normal pattern of development, but they are not functioning at an age-appropriate level when it comes to their speech or language skills. However, they may also be delayed in more than one area of development (for example, self-care, toileting, cognitive skills). In this case, their language delay is just part of their overall delayed development.

Speech and language delays can be associated with a history of child neglect. In child neglect, parents don't interact with children in the kind of reciprocal way that encourages language development and the development of a rich vocabulary.

However, language delays can also be caused by other factors associated with lack of access to medical care, such as repeated and chronic and untreated ear infections. Repeated and chronic ear infections significantly reduce children's ability to listen and learn from language input. Although it is difficult to generalize, children are often able to catch up in their delayed language skills – provided they receive early intervention and immersion in an enriching language environment and there are no medical reasons for the delayed development.

Speech and language disorders

The second form of difficulty that is associated with early adversity is some form of *speech and language disorder* (as opposed to speech and language *delay*). As the name suggests, this is a potentially more serious difficulty as it relates to the underlying processes of speech and language production. Children with this form of developmental difference can benefit from specific speech and language therapy.

The assessment and treatment of language disorders is complex and a thorough discussion of speech and language difficulties is beyond the scope of this book. This chapter should provide you with enough information to determine whether or not your child might have a speech and language difference. If this is indicated, your child will benefit from a referral to a speech therapist. So let's touch briefly on what speech and language difficulties look like, before moving on to looking at the strategies you might use to support a child with this form of developmental difference. The strategies in this chapter are not a substitute for professional speech and language therapy. However, they can help all children, irrespective of whether or not they have a formal diagnosis of language delay or language disorder. I describe the main types of speech and language disorders here so you can use this chapter as a focus of discussion if you decide that a referral to a speech pathologist is warranted.

SPEECH DISORDER

If your child has a speech disorder, you may notice they have difficulty in speaking with a clear voice; using a tone that makes speech interesting; speaking without hesitation, repetition or stuttering; or making the sounds of individual letters clearly enough that people can understand what is being said. Speech disorders are difficulties in the accurate production and expression of speech and its component sounds.

LANGUAGE DISORDER

If your child has a language disorder, you will find that they have difficulty in using words in the ways we expect in society. For example, your child might have difficulty in joining together individual words to make up a sentence; choosing and ordering their sentences to make up a story that makes sense and is correctly ordered; choosing the correct words to convey a desired meaning; or being able to make sense of what people are saying in context. Language disorders refer to the way we put words and sentences together to convey meaning, within the context of social interactions and social expectations.

COMMUNICATION DISORDER

If your child has a communication disorder, it means that they have difficulty in using language in different contexts and for different purposes. Children with communication difficulties don't necessarily have difficulty in knowing the words to use; but rather in *how to use words in social situations*.

Many children with communication disorders will have difficulty in understanding and complying with implicit language 'rules' that apply to the context we are in. For example, we understand that we talk differently around our family than we do when we talk to our boss. This reflects an understanding of the context and implicit social rules of language. We also have culture-specific, unwritten 'rules' of social conversation; for example, hold eye contact, take turns in talking and stay on the agreed topic of conversation.

One example of a communication disorder is *pragmatic* language disorder, in which children find it difficult to adapt their language to meet their social needs; they aren't able to use language in practical and social ways. Children with this difficulty may have trouble in taking turns or talk persistently but only on a narrow range of topics; they may have trouble understanding another's point of view. Children with this kind of difficulty don't really understand the implicit rules of how language is used socially. They may appear awkward, use overly formal language or have difficulty in joining in social conversations in a seamless way. Pragmatic language difficulties are common amongst children with FASD and ASD.

What kinds of problems will you notice with your child?

Speech and language difficulties are complex and only a professional speech therapist can conduct an assessment tailored to your child's needs. However, it can be helpful to think of speech and language difficulties in terms of the three main areas that are affected. Here's how I think about developmental difference in speech and language:

1. difficulty with receptive language (understanding what is being said to them)

2. difficulty with expressive language (difficulty in expressing themselves clearly and making themselves understood to others)

3. difficulty with social communication (finding it hard to use language practically and effectively in social situations).

In the remainder of this chapter, we'll look at each of these areas of difficulty in turn. Once again, we support children with this developmental difference using the same principles we use to support any other developmental difference. Namely:

- Modifying your expectations of your child (re-setting expectations to meet their current abilities). Remind yourself it's not that your child *won't*, it's that they *can't*.

- Modifying the environment to enable your child to be successful (simplifying and shortening interactions, using visual prompts, and modifying how you give instructions to children).

- Supporting your child to develop social and behavioural competence, by teaching them missing language and vocabulary skills.

Modifying your expectations of your child may mean using simplified language wherever possible (without embarrassing your child by using 'baby talk'). Expect to have to repeat yourself. Expect to use visual reminders and other support strategies.

Modifying the environment of a child with this developmental difference might involve a range of simple strategies to help your child to be successful. Make sure the environment is supportive by minimizing any unnecessary noise. Reduce your child's need to rely on verbal information by using visual prompts wherever possible; include colour coding of tasks; use cartoon social stories or picture books to show how to problem solve social situations; or use picture sequences to spell out clearly the steps needed to complete a task. Part of modifying the environment also includes changing the way you interact with your child. Use simplified language, short sentences and repetition. Model the use of appropriate self-talk in social situations (e.g. 'I'd better use my inside voice now so I'm not talking too loud'). Notice and reinforce the appropriate use of language. Allow time for your child to respond to your questions. Reflect back and expand on their communication to build their vocabulary.

Supporting your child's language development might involve teaching a range of vocabulary and word meanings, as well as the rules of the social use of language. Teach your child the names and meanings of feelings words to give them the emotional literacy and necessary language to deal with frustration (see Chapter 6 for additional strategies to build their emotional literacy). Teach children the words to let people know that they don't understand in a way that doesn't cause them embarrassment. Expect to have to 'spell out' your expectations in a step by step fashion, using visual prompts when needed, until your child is able to do things for themselves.

How do I tell if my child has a language or communication difficulty?

Here are some of the behaviours you might notice with each type of language and communication difficulty:

If your child has trouble understanding what is being said to them

If this is the case, you might notice the following behaviours:

- Your child seems to ignore what you ask them to do.

- You need to repeat yourself or show your child what you want them to do before they understand what they need to do.

- Your child may mimic or repeat what is said to them.

- They might do the wrong thing often because they didn't understand what you wanted.

- Your child might have difficulty understanding complex instructions but can manage if you use simpler words and shorter sentences.

- They might get frustrated or angry easily.

- The answers your child gives to questions seem to be 'off topic'.

- Your child may rely on others in a learning environment, copying others to mask their lack of understanding.

- They may have difficulty in following group conversations, avoiding or disrupting the group to mask their lack of understanding.

If you believe that your child has difficulty in understanding what people are saying, try these suggestions:

- Make sure you have your child's attention before trying to speak to them.

- Use your child's name and make sure they are looking at you (but don't force eye contact if they are not comfortable with that).

- Give short and simple instructions. Vary the tone in your voice to help them to pay attention to the important part of what you are saying.

- Give your instructions slowly, with emphasis, and with pauses between each element. Using pauses and intonation will help your child to attend to the important part of your instructions. For example, 'First...WASH your hands...(pause)...THEN set the table', or something similar. This might seem strange at first, but it will help your child to understand what's needed from them.

- If possible, back up your request by using gestures or pictures.

- Use concrete and unambiguous words; avoid abstract words or metaphors.

- Allow time for your child to process your request or instruction.

- Use simple questions, and avoid complex level questions (see the information about questioning 'levels' later in this chapter).

- Check for understanding. Ask your child to repeat back to you what you have asked them to do.

- Make an agreement with your child about how they signal to you that they don't understand, or that they're getting frustrated. This will give them a concrete alternative to whining or using challenging behaviour.

If your child has trouble making themselves understood by others

If your child has trouble in expressing themselves and making themselves understood by others, you might see the following behaviours:

- Your child uses short and simplistic sentences.

- Your child might rely on pointing or gestures to be understood.

- Your child might rely on a few familiar words and use these repeatedly.

- Your child may lack the language skills to join in a social group. They may appear shy or reserved.

- Your child gives explanations or tells stories that are hard to follow.

- Your child struggles in group situations such as classroom discussion. They have difficulty in keeping up with the pace of conversations.

- Your child can seem slow to express themselves. They may have difficulty in finding the right words to describe how they are feeling. They may rely on a lot of 'you knows' to fill gaps in their word knowledge.

- Your child may lack the words for expressing feelings, leading to inability to reflect on their emotions and the circumstances surrounding emotional events.

- Your child may frequently feel frustrated when not given enough time to express themselves.

If you believe that your child has difficulty in expressing themselves, try these suggestions:

- Slow down (count to 10) to ensure that you give your child enough time to respond to what you are asking. They will need time to think about what they want to say, find the right words, and put them in an order that makes sense. These are not automatic or effortless tasks for children with expressive language difficulty.

- Gently repeat back what your child says, using the correct words, grammar and sentence structure. This gives them the opportunity to hear what they are trying to say, but in the correct context.

- Gradually introduce new words and expand your child's current vocabulary. Respond to your child's communication by adding to, and expanding on, the word they have used (for example, by adding a descriptive word, or offering an alternative word). This is the way that children learn to expand their expressive vocabulary.

- Talking aloud is one way to build your child's language skills without putting undue pressure on them. For example, you could say 'I see you have painted three balloons' then 'What have you painted?' and 'What colours are those balloons? I think one is red and one is blue? I wonder what colour the other one is?' This kind of 'wondering aloud' provides your child a stress-free way to listen to language being used in the correct way and in the correct context.

- Try to avoid stepping in too soon to provide 'words' for your child when they are struggling because this doesn't help them in the long run. You might try instead offering prompts or forced choices to assist them, such as 'Is that a mouse or a rabbit?' Resist the temptation to finish your child's sentences for them, for similar reasons.

- However, make sure you are prepared to step in and rescue them if their language skills cause them social embarrassment. For example, if they need to play with new children, give them the words they need to say to ask if they can join in the group.

- Help your child prepare for language-reliant school tasks, especially those that risk social embarrassment. Many supposed 'enjoyable' activities at school actually rely on high level language skills. Examples include class 'show and tell' times or when children are asked to talk about what they did in the holidays. If your child's teacher insists they take part in these activities, you will need to prepare and rehearse these language-dense tasks with your child.

- Provide balance in your child's life by providing them with lots of opportunities to shine. Get them involved in tasks, activities and hobbies that don't rely on language to strengthen and support your child's 'star qualities'.

If your child has trouble in using language in practical and social ways

If your child has difficulty with the social use of language (social communication difficulty), you may notice the following behaviours:

- They may not be able to use language in all the ways expected of a child their age (to say hello, to ask for help, to give directions, to give instructions).

- Your child may have trouble adjusting their language to suit the context and the needs of their audience (for example, they may have difficulty in moderating their voice when they come indoors; or changing to 'polite' language when talking to a teacher; or in simplifying their language to suit a much younger child).

- Your child takes things very literally. They may have real trouble in understanding metaphors and jokes based on double meanings.

- Your child has not picked up the implicit 'rules' and social conventions of language. For example, they do not understand that you take turns in conversation or that you stick to the topic being discussed and don't re-direct conversation towards your own interests.

- Your child's voice might lack rhythm and may not vary in intonation or pace.

- You may find your child has difficulty in transferring and applying the social rules of conversation from one setting to another.

If you suspect that your child has difficulty with a communication disorder, try these strategies:

- You will need to teach your child the *actual words* to use in common social situations. Whereas most children will pick up social conventions automatically, your child won't pick this up by themselves and will need explicit teaching. Examples of unspoken social conventions include what to say when greeting someone; how to announce you are leaving and say goodbye; how to start a conversation with someone; how to ask for help; how to ask to join a social group; how to address a teacher or a neighbour.

- Practise 'noticing' how conversations and social interactions happen; for example, by watching movies together. Teach your child the 'rules' of conversation and turn taking in particular.

- Encourage your child to practise giving eye contact, or intermittent eye contact, to the extent that they are able and willing. Many children who have ASD or who have been severely mistreated may have difficulty in giving eye contact but they should be encouraged (not forced) to give eye contact to the level they are able. Some children who are uncomfortable with eye contact can nonetheless learn to look at others' eyebrows or nose – which is often more acceptable to other children in their social group than breaking the 'unwritten rule' of giving eye contact, by your child refusing to look at someone they are talking to.

The resources section at the back of this book has websites and resources that can be helpful if you suspect that your child has a communication disorder.

Questioning children with speech and language difficulties

One of the challenges in supporting a child with language delay or language disorder is getting them to reflect on their behaviour and to problem solve social difficulties. When we ask a child to reflect on their behaviour (typically when they are in trouble) we are actually asking them to engage in a very complex cognitive and language activity.

Children with speech and language difficulties have difficulty in reflecting on their behaviour and coming up with solutions to social problems because of limited language and cognitive skills. This includes the ability to think about a problem from another person's point of view, the ability to predict the consequences of their actions and the ability to describe possible alternative behaviours. These skills all require abstract thinking and high level language skills. A child's difficulty in reflecting on their behaviour reflects their language compromise and not their deliberate defiance.

We can help children to reflect on their behaviour by simplifying the language aspect of this conversation. One way to support children in reflecting on their behaviour is to change the way that we question them about it. Researchers in the 1970s identified four different types of questions that range from simple to complex (see Box 6).

Asking a child to reflect on their behaviour typically involves the most complex type of questions that need high level language skills. When we ask children why they behaved a certain way or what they could have done differently we are asking them the most complex kind of questions. These researchers found that a child's ability to answer complex questions depends on them having mastered the easier level questions (reflecting simpler language skills). Children with language difficulties will struggle with the more complex and reflective questions. Asking them simpler level questions will make it easier for them to take part in conversations about their behaviour. As much as possible, try to use the simpler questions in your interactions with your child (see Box 6).

BOX 6
Choosing questions that your child can understand

Here I give samples of questions to ask children (adapted from Blank, Rose and Berlin, 1978 and McLean, 2017). These are organized according to their level of complexity. Children with language difficulties should *only be asked the simpler level questions* in order to avoid frustration. Complex questions can only be understood once a child has mastered the necessary language to understand simpler questions. Supplement questions with visual prompts or cartoon pictures wherever possible.

Level 1 questions
The simplest questions are ones that ask a child to directly report what they have seen or heard. The majority of preschool children can understand and respond to this type of question, and we should use these as much as possible.

Examples include:

'What's this?' or 'What did you see?'

These questions ask children about tangible things that they can see, hear or touch.

Level 2 questions

Questions at the next level are slightly more complex, and ask a child to describe, analyse and reflect about an object's purpose or characteristics. The majority of preschool children can understand and respond to this type of question. These kinds of questions can be used with most children with language difficulties.

Examples include:

'What's happening in this picture?' or 'What things did the man say to do?'

Level 3 questions

The next level questions are more complex involving more abstract and less concrete questions. Children will find this kind of question difficult unless they have mastered the simpler types of questions first. This kind of question is not just about tangible things that a child can see, touch and hear; it asks them to make predictions and generalizations, to understand how things are ordered or to take another's perspective. Children with language difficulty will not be able to understand this kind of question – yet these are the types of questions we typically ask them in relation to their behaviour.

Examples include:

'What will happen next?' or 'How would Jonny do that?' or 'How are these two situations similar?'

Level 4 questions

Questions at this level are the most complex kinds of questions. They involve problem solving, reasoning about their experiences and offering predictions and explanations. Most five-year-olds can understand this kind of question, but children with language difficulties won't be able to follow them.

Examples include:

'What will happen if you push Jonny?' or 'Why can't you run inside?' or 'How can you tell Jonny is sad?' or 'What could you do to fix this situation?'

For more information about questions and their complexity see The Language of Learning: The Preschool Years by Blank et al., 1978; or 'Foster parent's guide to language and communication difficulties' by McLean, 2017.

Chapter 6

Developmental Difference in Emotional Regulation

In this chapter, we'll look at one of the key reasons why children have difficulty with behaviour: namely delays and difficulty with emotional regulation. This developmental difference is common amongst children who have experienced a range of early adversities. First, let's explore what we mean by the impact of early adversity on healthy emotional development and what emotional regulation difficulties are.

Healthy emotional development is the foundation of friendship, stronger social connections and better educational outcomes. Children who value emotions and express emotions in socially acceptable ways tend to be more popular, have better relationships and friendships, have better coping skills and experience more well-being throughout their lives. One of the best gifts that we can give our children is to value, accept and express their emotions in socially acceptable ways.

Children's emotional development can be set off course because of their early life experience. There are some significant reasons for this. Let's look at some of the reasons why children learn to devalue or ignore emotions.

Delayed emotional development

First, children's emotional development can become *delayed*. This can happen if a child's family of origin wasn't able to provide the necessary environment for a child to develop emotional intelligence. If a child's early environment was characterized by neglect; or if emotions weren't valued by their family members, then it is not surprising that their knowledge about emotions and how to manage them may be delayed.

A child who has delayed emotional development may seem much younger than their actual age in their ability to talk about feelings, or to understand another's feelings. It is common for children in care to have delayed emotional development and delayed emotional vocabulary when they enter care. This kind of difficulty usually responds to a supportive and enriching home environment that models and values safe emotional expression.

Disavowed emotions

Second, some children have learned that emotions are unsafe. As a result, they 'shut down' on some emotions and are no longer able to easily access these feelings. It is common for a child from an abusive home to have the experience of being ridiculed or humiliated for expressing 'vulnerable' emotions like sadness or fear. To avoid the 'shame' of being ridiculed, a child learns not to show emotions that they associate with being ashamed.

Another example is when a child is punished for expressing anger towards a parent. If this happens often enough, the child very quickly learns that they have to supress angry feelings in order to remain safe. Similarly, if a child has experienced overwhelming fear and terror in the context of a trauma, they can 'shut down' the expression of fear because this reminds them of their trauma. If this happens often, they can over-rely on 'shutting down' or 'cutting off' from feelings as a means of 'coping by avoidance'. Over time, if this continues, a child can develop difficulty in expressing *any* emotions, even positive ones.

There are many good reasons why children from abusive and neglectful environments become 'shut off' from their feelings, when these emotions become 'unsafe' in the child's mind. These children need support to learn that it is safe to express emotions.

Distorted emotions

Third, children can learn to distort or re-direct their emotions in order to secure their parent's attention and affection. In a 'typical' family, a child learns that they can express emotions freely and these emotions can be tolerated by their caregiver. A child's caregiver helps them to manage overwhelming emotions by naming and co-regulating strong emotions with them until they are old enough to develop the capacity to self-regulate their emotions. In this way, a child learns that feelings are safe to share; are manageable; and are temporary. These are important early lessons about the value and safety of emotions.

If a child's caregiver does not reliably respond to their emotional signals, they learn a very different lesson about emotions. In abusive or neglectful caregiving, a child learns that expressing their feelings is not enough to elicit care from their caregiver. In this case, a child can learn to *distort their feelings* in order to make sure that their caregiver responds. A child with this kind of background learns to dismiss, minimize or exaggerate their authentic emotion so that feelings are tolerated by their caregiver.

In other words, in abnormal caregiving situations, a child learns that the expression of their authentic feelings is only conditionally accepted by their caregiver. They learn to distort, minimize or exaggerate their emotions to make them acceptable to adults. For example, a child might learn to exaggerate or escalate their distress in order to get a response from their caregiver. Alternatively, a child might learn to minimize or suppress their distress so that their caregiver isn't angered by their demands. This can sometimes appear to others to be manipulative; however, in most cases a child isn't aware of the fact that they are distorting their authentic emotions.

What skills need strengthening for a child with poor emotional regulation?

For a range of reasons, children whose emotions have not been tolerated, encouraged or valued have difficulty with emotional regulation. They don't develop a healthy range of emotions and don't have healthy ways to express their authentic emotions and needs. As a result, children in care are likely to need more support than other children to understand their emotions and to recognize, describe, express and manage them.

If your child has developmental difference in their ability for emotional regulation, there are three main areas of skill that they will need support with. These are:

1. building your child's ability to recognize and name emotions (building their emotional literacy)

2. building your child's understanding of the connection between their feelings and their bodily sensations (their body–mind connection)

3. building your child's ability to regulate and express emotions in socially acceptable ways.

If your child struggles with any of these areas of emotional regulation, they are also more likely to have social and behavioural difficulties. Typically, we'd look at building emotional literacy first, followed by their understanding of the body–mind connection, then finally look at emotional regulation skills. Let's look at each of these areas in turn.

Building your child's ability to recognize and name emotions

The first skill that children need to have in order to manage emotions effectively is the ability to recognize emotions. While this sounds obvious, many children in care do not have basic emotional literacy. They do not have a language or a vocabulary for feelings. Without a repertoire of feeling words it is impossible for your child to take part in conversations about feelings. Children need a language for talking about emotions. Helping your child to build a feelings vocabulary will be an important first step towards enabling them to recognize feelings, talk about them and develop emotion regulation skills.

Many children in care are delayed when it comes to their emotional literacy. A child's emotional literacy refers to their ability to recognize emotions in themselves and others and to describe these emotions to others. It is the foundation for emotional development. Children's emotional literacy develops well in families in which feelings are valued, and feelings words are used in conversation. In the absence of these kinds of early experiences, children can experience delays in this area.

If your child has poor emotional literacy, you may notice that they lack the words to describe how they feel. Your child may have a very limited, and basic, range of feeling words. Your child may show very little awareness of what they, or others, are feeling. Your child may not appear to register their emotions. In extreme cases, your child may not cry when injured, or have difficulty in recognizing their own bodily reactions as signals of emotion (for example, they can't equate an upset tummy with feeling afraid).

For these children it is important to go 'back to basics'. Make it a priority to build your child's emotional vocabulary and their ability to recognize and name feelings. Children who do not have the vocabulary necessary to express their feelings will resort to communicating through behaviour. For very young children, the emphasis should be on learning the basic feelings words (happy, sad, scared, angry), and on learning about feelings as part of play. Here are some suggestions for building your child's emotional literacy:

- Start with the basic emotions. You can support this process by providing a range of toys that can be used to convey different emotions. For example, use 'angry' animals like lions and tigers, 'scary' animals like spiders and snakes, and 'loving, happy' animals like rabbits or cats. These can provide a natural way to incorporate feeling words into your child's play. Once they understand the basic feeling words, you can expand your child's vocabulary by extending their basic feelings vocabulary when the opportunity arises (for example, the basic feeling word 'scared' can be extended to 'worried', 'nervous' or 'frightened').

• Another way to introduce feelings to young children is to involve them in making feelings 'flashcards'. Feelings flashcards can be made from drawings, magazine pictures or photos that depict a range of feelings. Have your child find pictures from old story books, magazines or newspapers that identify different feelings. Start with simple emotions (happy, sad, angry). Help your child to play detective. Get them to identify the parts of the face or the body that let them know what feeling is being depicted. As the child gets more comfortable with this task, you can widen the number of feelings cards you include. You can also try a variation of this task when you collect pictures of people and groups and together look at the clues that tell you how the people in the pictures are feeling. (What do their eyes look like? What are their hands doing? Are they smiling or frowning?)

• Young children can also enjoy playing a game of 'feelings faces'. Take it in turns to pull 'feelings faces'. See if your child can guess how you are feeling. Draw their attention to one or two facial features that help them to guess what you are feeling. Ask them what kinds of things make people have this kind of feelings face. Have your child take a turn to pretend to show an emotion on their face (they might like to have a mirror to use to watch their reflection as they do so). Offer one or two guesses about what might make them feel happy or sad and share with them the clues that helped you guess how they were feeling.

School-age children can tolerate more structured and complex discussions about feelings, especially when you include these discussions as a natural part of their play or daily activities:

- You can use your child's favourite TV shows or story books as opportunities to practise identifying the emotions in the different characters and to understand what makes a character feel the way they do. This can help them to take another's perspective. The capacity to do this is an important social skill that is linked to strong social and peer relationships later in life. You might start a conversation about their favourite character. Ask your child what might have led the story character to feel that way. Ask if that character always feels (happy, sad), or do they sometimes have other feelings? Ask how the character copes with bad feelings and helps themselves to feel better. In this way, you can slowly extend your child's ability to imagining how others are feeling, to recognize others' feelings and to understand that feelings (even bad feelings) don't last forever.

- Teenagers are generally more able to engage in conversation about feelings and inner emotions and thoughts, depending on their developmental level. Adolescents can benefit from watching you model a healthy attitude towards emotions and towards expressing feelings in a socially acceptable way. However, many adolescents may also have already developed unhelpful ways of denying or managing strong emotions and may benefit from additional professional support to explore their feelings and their default coping style.

Building your child's understanding of the body-mind connection

Many children need support with making the connection between their bodily sensations and what they are thinking and feeling. This is called our *body–mind connection*; and understanding this connection is an important part of learning to manage our emotions. Many children need extra support to understand what this connection looks like for them. They may not have been taught the link between what is happening in their *mind* (their thoughts and feelings) and what they are *experiencing* in their bodies.

So what do we mean by the body–mind connection?

Our understanding of the body–mind connection is something we take for granted. We know that when we feel stressed our body signals us in important ways. We have learned to pay attention to these messages from our bodies. We might get sweaty palms, a dry mouth or a racing heart. Because we understand this connection, we know that if our palms suddenly get sweaty or our heart starts to race, there is probably something happening that we need to prepare for. Our bodies act as our early warning signals, providing us with very important information that we need to act on. We take the bodily sensations associated with fear very seriously.

A child's body also gives them clues that they are feeling angry or afraid. For some children in care, however, this important early warning sign doesn't work well. Sometimes children haven't made this connection for themselves; sometimes they learn to ignore this connection because of their early experiences and sometimes this connection becomes 'wired' in a distorted way.

Some children have learned to ignore their body–emotion connection. For example, children who have been neglected may become 'disconnected' from bodily sensations. They learn to 'cut off' feelings or bodily sensations like hunger or thirst because these signals were consistently ignored by their caregivers. These are the children that may not cry when they are injured. It's almost as though their body no longer registers pain. Children who have experienced physical and sexual abuse may also have learned to 'shut off' attention to their body signals, bodily sensations and their feelings. Other children that can become 'desensitized' to bodily signals are those that have lived in an environment of constant fear and vigilance. In short, there are a range of very good reasons why children in care may have become less sensitive to their body–feelings connection.

Other children may become over-sensitized to their bodily sensations, mis-interpreting bodily sensations and their meanings. For example, exercise can trigger panic reactions in some children. This is because the increase in heart rate that comes with exercise reminds them of past trauma and fear (when fear caused increased heart rate). These children need support to accurately discriminate between bodily signals that signal danger and those that are 'false alarms'. Some children have difficulty in recognizing when their body is relaxed and calm; these sensations feel foreign initially. These children may need to practise feeling calm and peaceful until it begins to feel normal to them.

In other children, this body–mind connection becomes distorted. These children may experience somatic symptoms like headaches or stomach aches. These symptoms can be manifestations of unrecognized or unexpressed feelings, particularly anger and fear (although possible medical causes should be investigated first).

If your child has any of these difficulties, they will need your support to make the connection between what they are feeling in their bodies and the emotions they are experiencing. One of the most powerful ways to teach children about this is to model your understanding of this connection in your own body. 'Talking aloud' about your experiences can help children make this connection in their own bodies for themselves (for example, 'My hands are shaking, I must be getting nervous').

If your child has a lot of somatic symptoms, it may take longer for them to make the connection between their bodily sensations and their feelings. If your child frequently complains of a stomach ache or a headache, try gently introducing the idea that 'Sometimes our body tells us how we are feeling, if we learn to listen to it.' For example, you can say 'Sometimes our body tells us we are scared by giving us tummy aches or making our tummies feel like they are full of butterflies. When that happens to me I know it is my body telling me I am afraid and I need to ask for help.' It is important not to dismiss these symptoms, but accept them as the only real way your child has of showing you their emotional pain at this time. Over time, when these symptoms are accepted and normalized, your child will come to better accept their own emotions and make the connection between their bodily sensations and their emotions. Of course, you will need to rule out medical causes for your child's physical symptoms before you can assume they are emotional in nature.

There are also simple activities you can do with your child that can help to introduce the connection between bodily sensations and feelings. The first of these is a variation on the 'feelings face' game described earlier. In this activity you create a template of a blank face by drawing a large face outline on a piece of card or paper. Ask your child to think of a time when they felt a certain emotion (happy, sad, angry) and encourage them to show how this emotion affected their face, by drawing these features onto the template. For example, your child might draw in scrunched eyebrows, squinting eyes, tightness in the forehead or flushed cheeks. Ask your child to explain 'What does this feeling do to your eyes?' or 'How does this feeling make your cheeks feel?' Your child may like to colour in and keep their 'happy', 'angry' and 'sad' feelings faces. You can use these pictures as a prompt for discussion when these feelings arise in the future.

Another useful activity is a body paint exercise. For this activity, create a body shape outline on a large piece of butcher's paper. Have your child identify and colour in the areas of their body that correspond with various feelings. For example, you could ask them to use blue paint or crayon to colour the areas of their body that are affected when they feel sad. You can then repeat this exercise using red crayon for angry feelings (the colour is not important; follow your child's lead with this). You can use this opportunity to normalize the body–mind connection. Explain how everyone's feelings affect their bodies in some way and that our bodies give us very important clues about how we feel.

Build your child's ability to regulate and express emotions in socially acceptable ways

If your child has developmental difference in capacity for emotional regulation, they will also need support to regulate and express their emotions in a socially acceptable and appropriate way. It is worth emphasizing again here that your child's ability to manage and regulate their emotions is really based on them having developed the earlier skill of emotional literacy and on them understanding the connection between their feelings and bodily sensations. Put simply, your child needs to have learned to recognize and talk about feelings before you can expect them to learn to tolerate and manage these feelings.

The key learning for your child in learning the skill of emotional regulation is your child's understanding that they can 'be the boss' of their feelings rather than their feelings being the boss of them. In other words, let your child know that, just like adults, children can learn 'tricks' to cope with feelings.

There are a few steps you can take to support your child to develop the skills to manage and regulate emotions.

- First, support your child by reflecting back their feelings to them. Respond to your child's feelings by using feelings words that reflect their experience back to them. For example, say 'You feel really angry right now' or 'You feel very sad that you can't go out because it's raining.' Reflecting back feelings helps your child to connect with that feeling. This is something that can be difficult for them to do in the heat of the moment and when feelings are overwhelming them. Reflecting back what you think they are feeling will help your child to strengthen their body–mind connection. It doesn't hurt to guess, even if you're not sure what your child is feeling. Making the effort to understand shows them that feelings are valued.

- When emotions are running high, it is best to use short, simple sentences to reflect your child's feelings. If their arousal level is high, it will be difficult for them to process what you are telling them, especially if you use long sentences or give them too much information. If your child is in the midst of a meltdown, short instructions are most effective. These should focus on what behaviour you want them to do in order to calm down. Tell your child what to do rather than what to stop doing. This makes all the difference. How often have you heard a parent tell a distressed and wound-up child to 'Stop running in the house!' It's so much more effective to tell them what to do: 'Go and jump on the trampoline.'

- You may also need to teach your child co-regulation and coping strategies. Introduce and model the use of coping strategies to your child. For example, 'When I get angry I like to go for a run with the dog' or 'When I am sad I hug the dog.' It can help your child enormously to provide them with two positive choices for coping when they are in the middle of strong emotions, because it means they don't need to generate ideas for themselves when they are already feeling stressed. For example, you could say 'I can see you are angry. Do you want to jump on the trampoline or go kick the ball?' The goal is to convey to your child that strong feelings are normal and that adults have tricks for managing strong feelings when they come along.

- Your child will also have natural preferences in how they like to calm and self-soothe. Some have a strong preference for engaging in physical activity. Some prefer to take time to themselves to do a quiet activity. You will get to know your child's preferences over time. If your child prefers to engage in physical activity, you may like to keep a basket of bouncy balls, frisbees or foam bats by the back door so they can grab them and head outside to let off steam. Your child may prefer to calm down by taking alone time. If this is your child's preference, they may like you to create a corner with soft cushions or a makeshift 'chill-out' tent or tree house to hide away in for a while. Remind your child of their calming strategy when you can see them escalating. You may find it useful to rehearse your child's strategy with them ahead of time.

- Children can also learn to use relaxation skills and coping self-talk in times of stress. Your child can use stress reducing breathing techniques when their emotions threaten to overwhelm them. Deep, steady breathing is extremely soothing; deep breathing changes the body chemistry from 'fight or flight' to a calm state. Teach your child to take two to three deep breaths when the going gets tough. Deep breathing is a fast, easy to use and transportable calming strategy. Younger children can be encouraged to use deep, slow breaths to imagine that they are blowing an imaginary bubble or blowing up an imaginary balloon.

- You can also teach your child coping self-talk such as, 'It's OK, I'm safe now', 'I can get through this' or 'I'll just do my deep breathing.' Practise your child's chosen regulation and calming strategy with them ahead of time at a time when they are feeling reasonably calm. Think of this practice as like conducting a 'fire drill' – something that needs to be rehearsed so that it is 'automatic' during times of stress when it is needed.

- Many children also find it useful to develop a 'feelings box'. Children who aren't willing to talk about their feelings with you may be willing to use a feelings box to help regulate their feelings. This box can contain objects that your child feels are useful in calming; for example, a foam stress ball for angry feelings, a picture of a loved one or a soft toy for comfort. Some children prefer a 'coping tool box' in which they place reminders of what they can do to make themselves feel better; for example, a card that says 'Hug the dog' or 'Listen to music'.

BOX 7

A note about the impact of trauma and dissociation on children's emotional regulation

Some children will need professional support and therapy in addition to the ideas presented in this chapter. If your child has experienced prolonged or severe trauma, they will benefit from a referral for specialized trauma therapy to support them to process their feelings.

Extreme traumatic events can cause a child to 'shut off' from their feelings to protect themselves from overwhelming terror. While this protective strategy made a lot of sense during times of intolerable fear, it can become entrenched as a persistent way of coping over time. In this case, a child can become chronically disconnected from, and unaware of, their feelings. These children can come to rely on 'tuning out' or dissociating from events in their daily life as a means of coping. They will benefit from professional support to make the journey to accepting and expressing their emotions in healthy ways.

Chapter 7

Developmental Difference in Executive Functioning

In this chapter, we'll look at one of the key reasons why children have difficulty with learning and behaviour: namely their impaired executive functioning and executive control. This developmental difference is common amongst children with a range of clinical disorders, but we believe it is also common amongst children who have experienced early adversity. First, let's explore what we mean by executive functioning and executive functioning difficulties.

Executive functioning and children's behaviour

We believe that children who have experienced early adversity have impaired executive functioning. This is significant because all social behaviour and learning is underpinned by the brain's executive functioning skills.

Impaired executive functioning affects your child's ability to control their attention, draw on their memory and focus their attention towards planning and carrying out complex tasks. The executive functioning skills are a collection of interrelated cognitive skills that are involved in virtually every task involving memory, attention, sustained focus and learning. This is why executive functioning skills are so important for everyday life and why this form of developmental difference has such an impact on a child's life.

When a child's executive functioning skills are not working together in a synchronized and coordinated way, we say that a child has poor 'executive control'. Executive control is like the 'air traffic controller' or 'orchestra conductor' of the brain. The role of the executive control centre is to ensure that the various executive functioning skills work seamlessly together to ensure the brain's smooth and coordinated functioning. Without the 'executive control centre' of the brain working efficiently our thinking, memory, approach to learning and behaviour can be disorganized, erratic or seem out of context (think of what would happen if an orchestra lost its conductor or an airport tried to function without an experienced air traffic controller!). Executive control – and the executive functioning skills that underpin this – is absolutely central to your child's success in academic, work and social settings.

In this chapter we'll discuss some of the principal skills of executive functioning and look at how to support the key executive skills, so that your child's ability for executive control is optimized. We don't need to understand exactly how the various executive skills work together in order to be able to support a child (this is a topic that scientists disagree on and continue to debate). We just need to help strengthen those executive functioning skills that are key to children's success in social and educational settings.

BOX 8

Child development and executive control

Children's capacity for executive control depends on their age. It's important to note that it is entirely normal for young (preschool age) children to have underdeveloped executive control. We think that by the time a child is seven or eight, however, there is a marked increase in the efficiency of their executive control system.

Scientists are still developing their understanding of how executive functioning skills develop and interact with each other to shape a child's behaviour. We do know, however, that there is a relationship between impaired executive functioning and childhood behaviour disorders, across all age groups (Martel *et al.*, 2017). Difficulties with one or more executive skills are commonly found in children with persistent behaviour problems and with other difficulties in social and educational functioning. Delayed executive control can become obvious in school-age children who have disruptive behaviour and difficulty in concentration and attention.

The difference between your child's actual age and their developmental age (executive functioning) can be marked. Therefore, it is more realistic to align your expectations with your child's developmental age rather than their actual age.

What are the executive functioning skills?

Executive functioning skills underpin smooth executive control. The exact nature and interrelationship of these skills is the subject of ongoing research. Most researchers agree that there are several key skills that affect children's behaviour and learning. In non-technical terms, we can think of smooth executive control as being made up of four main areas of executive skills. One or more of the following skills are likely to be compromised in children with behavioural, social or learning difficulties. We'll look at strategies to support each of these skills a little later in this chapter. If your child has difficulty with any of these areas, you might find the strategies helpful.

Difficulty with getting started, planning and organizing

Your child may have trouble *getting started* on an activity ('warming up' to or initiating a task). A child with this difficulty can't seem to organize their thoughts enough to know how to get started on a task. This difficulty can often be interpreted as laziness, procrastination or lack of motivation. Children who have this difficulty can become so overwhelmed by working out how and where to start a task that they end up doing nothing. They never start anything because they can't work out where to begin! This is often interpreted as defiance or lack of motivation.

Your child may have also trouble with *planning, organizing and monitoring* their performance during an activity. This involves difficulty with breaking a task into smaller steps and smaller goals and keeping track of their progress towards their end goal. A child with this difficulty can struggle to keep track of belongings and may be constantly losing things. Once started on a task, they may lose track easily, easily go off topic or get distracted due to their difficulty in monitoring what they are doing.

Difficulty with working memory

Your child may have difficulty with *working memory*. Your working memory is a type of 'short-term' memory that you draw on when trying to keep important information in the forefront of your mind. If your child has this difficulty, they may appear forgetful, or they may seem at times as though they are not paying attention. They may struggle to remember instructions, especially multi-step instructions, and have difficulty in remembering instructions long enough to complete a task. It is extremely common for teachers to misinterpret this difficulty as deliberate non-compliance.

Difficulty with flexible thinking

Your child may have difficulty with *cognitive flexibility* (flexible thinking). The child with this difficulty seems to get stuck on one way of doing things. They find it hard to respond and adapt their behaviour even when given feedback that their behaviour is inappropriate, annoying or creating problems for others. They find it difficult to change what they are doing – even if it isn't working. Children with this difficulty can't easily come up with alternative solutions and find it difficult to change strategy once they start on a task (they seem to become 'stuck' in one way of doing things, even if it doesn't work). They can also find transitioning from task to task difficult and will need additional support such as time warnings, visual prompts and task lists to support them to leave one activity and start a new one. This difficulty is often evident in children who struggle in unstructured settings or in moving from one activity to another.

Difficulty with emotional and behavioural control

Your child may have trouble with *emotional and behavioural control*. If this is the case, your child's emotional or behavioural outbursts may seem extreme: they often over-react emotionally, and in response to what seem minor triggers. Children with poor emotional control can also be impulsive. An impulsive child has great difficulty in checking their actions, often rushing through tasks quickly.

On the other extreme, children with emotional control problems can also have difficulty in recognizing and expressing emotions appropriately. These children may under-react emotionally in situations that we might expect them to find upsetting. Some children have difficulty in expressing *any* feelings at all, even when these feelings are appropriate to the circumstances. Difficulties with emotional and behavioural control can result in either over-reactive or under-reactive children.

The 'hallmark' features of compromised executive control

If you are unsure about whether or not your child might benefit from strategies to build their executive skills, ask yourself if your child exhibits these two 'hallmark' features of children with compromised executive control:

- *Difficulty with unstructured activities:* consider how well your child manages unstructured settings, when compared with more structured settings. Children with executive functioning difficulty tend to cope well in highly structured and predictable settings but have difficulty in unstructured or unpredictable settings. So it's common for a child with this kind of difficulty to have trouble with playtimes and lunch breaks or in large group activities where the potential for unpredictable interactions is large.

- *Difficulty with transitions of all kinds:* consider how well your child copes with transitioning from one activity to another. Children with executive functioning difficulty tend to have difficulty in transitions of all kinds. This includes transitioning from activity to activity, from home to school or from classroom to classroom. A child with executive functioning difficulty will need additional support to make successful transitions, including pre-warning and anxiety management strategies.

If your child is experiencing difficulty in unstructured activities where expectations are unclear or in transitioning between activities and settings, then this chapter is likely to be relevant to you.

BOX 9

Is poor executive functioning always a sign that a child has been abused?

Many children in adoptive and foster care also need support with executive functioning. We know that children who have experienced early adversity, early brain damage, prenatal exposure to alcohol or severe maltreatment during childhood are prone to these types of executive difficulties (McLean and McDougall, 2014). If your child is experiencing executive functioning difficulties, it does not mean they have experienced abuse or neglect; executive functioning difficulties are common in many childhood disorders.

If your child has any of the following diagnoses, they are likely to have difficulty in one or more aspects of executive control: ASD;

ADHD; conduct disorder; oppositional defiant disorder; FASD; bipolar disorder; and any of the mood or anxiety disorders.

Children with ASD can have difficulty with forward planning, goal setting and self-regulation, and can be rigid and inflexible in their thinking and language. Children with a diagnosis of ADHD are more likely to have difficulty with behavioural inhibition (inhibiting inappropriate behaviour) and sustaining attention to task. Children with FASD are likely to have difficulty with working memory, with shifting attention from task to task and in transitioning from one activity to another. If your child has one of these diagnoses, you may find this chapter useful.

Some people argue that executive functioning difficulties are also common in children who have experienced abuse. We don't know for sure how abuse is related to poor executive control. We believe that brain development is altered in children who experience abuse (McLean, 2016b and Sattler 2016). The brain areas involved in detecting danger and responding to threat (the 'fight or flight' response) may become relatively more developed than executive functioning areas because of chronic experiences of being 'unsafe'. In an environment of chronic stress, 'threat detection' areas of the brain may become more 'developed' than areas involved in planning, thinking and reflection, as these 'executive control' areas of the brain develop much later. This may explain why children who have experienced abusive caregiving can have more difficulty in controlling behaviour and in organizing their thoughts and paying attention.

What might help your child?

We think that efficient executive control relies on the strength, efficiency and coordination of all the skills outlined above (Espy and Kaufmann, 2002). A child with executive control difficulties can struggle with one – or all – of the above skills. Their difficulties may be mild or extreme. We don't have specific tests that tell us which difficulties to focus on. We believe that we can help children with this developmental difference by using the same principles we use to support any other developmental difference. Namely:

- Modifying your expectations of your child (re-setting expectations to meet their current abilities). Think in terms of their 'developmental age', not their actual age. Remind yourself it's not that your child *won't* do what you ask, it's that they *can't.*

- Modifying and 'scaffolding' the environment to enable your child to be successful (this involves creating as much structure as possible; supporting transitions of any kind; simplifying and shortening interactions, using visual prompts, and modifying how you give instructions to children who may have memory difficulties).

- Supporting your child to develop social and behavioural competence, by supporting the development of their executive skills, using the suggestions in this chapter.

Let's look at how to recognize and respond to each of the main areas of executive functioning difficulty next: planning and organization, memory, flexible thinking and behavioural control.

Supporting the child with difficulty in planning and organization skills

Children who experience difficulty in this area have trouble in getting started on a task, in planning and organizing themselves and in keeping themselves on track (self-monitoring so they don't get distracted). They can find it hard to plan and prioritize the steps in a task (for example, the steps involved in learning for a test).

These kinds of difficulties tend to be most noticeable in a school setting and children who experience planning and organization difficulties often come to the attention of their teacher. A child with this kind of difficulty can seem as though they lack ambition, are unmotivated, lazy or forgetful. Many children 'act-out' in a school environment to avoid letting others know they are having difficulty in keeping up.

These children may need an adult to provide structure. It is common for children to give up on schoolwork, finding it too overwhelming. They may need one on one support from an adult to keep them on track, remind them of the next steps and help them break down schoolwork into manageable chunks. In other words, provide the child with a sense of structure. Children with this kind of difficulty find school increasingly difficult as they get older and are expected to be more self-directed in their learning. This difficulty often means a child will struggle to set goals of any sort without support (e g. saving money for a toy or practising music skills for a performance).

The following are clues that planning and organization might be difficult for your child:

- Your child doesn't know where or how to start a task or is slow to get started.

- Your child is not able to organize tasks or set goals on their own.

- Your child has difficulty with multi-step tasks and seems to lose place or lose focus.

- Your child is not able to plan ahead or predict consequences of actions.

- Your child is not able to prioritize and is easily distracted by irrelevant activities.

- Your child is not able to keep track of belongings or keep their school bag and room tidy.

- Your child is not able to follow age-appropriate routines independently.

- Your child never allows enough time to complete school assignments.

- Your child needs supervision to stay on task and complete activities.

We can help children with this kind of difficulty by reducing the demands we place on their executive functioning skills, principally by providing structure and routine and clear step by step instructions. If you think that difficulties in organization and planning might be a problem for your child, try the following strategies:

- Try to provide a simplified, structured and uncluttered environment, with clear routines and where your expectations are spelled out explicitly and simply.

- It can be helpful to have key routines demonstrated as visual sequences, using cartoons or photos to show your child the steps in daily routine. Examples of important daily routines that your child might need visual prompts and supports for include:

  - bedtime routines (bath, brush teeth, put on pyjamas, read a story, lights out)

  - getting ready for school (eat breakfast, brush teeth, put on uniform, pack schoolbag)

  - coming in from school (empty school bag, put uniform in wash, have snack, play time, start homework).

- Use colour coding to help categorize your child's tasks and chores (using specific coloured bins for toys and for shoes, dirty washing, etc.). Use visual reminders and prompts.

- Involve your child in organizing their bedroom so that they know where everything goes. Use the same approach to children's belongings (e.g. school bag, wardrobe).

- Use lists wherever possible, and teach your child to use lists effectively. Lists should spell out the steps needed to complete in sequence.

- You may need to support your child to manage time more effectively. It can be useful to set a time limit for each step in a project so your child doesn't become 'stuck' on any one step. Older children may prefer to use a phone app or online organization tools for the same purpose, although they will still need your support initially.

- Use a 'zoning' system. Have clearly defined places for specific things (e.g. where to put school bag, a place for recharging phone and laptop, specific sleeves or coloured folders for each school subject).

- Break big tasks down into smaller jobs and make your expectations for each step clear; monitor children's progress, providing prompts for next steps if needed, and provide positive feedback for staying on task.

- Mind mapping tools can help your child to map out all the steps in a project and to make a visual representation of how concepts connect to one another. These can be a helpful support to children to help them switch between 'big picture' and sequential thinking.

- Provide a role model to your child by modelling the self-talk that you use to help yourself to stay on task. For example, you might talk aloud when you're doing something, to provide your child with a role model about how to keep on track (e.g. 'What am I'm supposed to next?'; 'How many steps to go now?').

Supporting the child with difficulty in working memory

Our 'working memory' is our ability to temporarily hold and manipulate information in our minds, while at the same time performing a task that draws on this information. Our working memory underpins many of the activities we do in day-to-day life; for example, we rely on our working memory when we are asked to recite a telephone number that we've just heard. Working memory underpins any task that requires sustained focus, such as schoolwork.

There are many 'tricks' we use to strengthen our working memory. In the example I gave above about reciting a telephone number, we could 'rehearse' the number in our minds so that we don't forget it. Or we could 'chunk' the number to make it easier to remember. This strategy allows us to cram more numbers into our working memory system. We often take for granted this amazing part of our brain's processing. Children who have experienced early adversity may not be able to access their working memory as easily as other children.

If your child has poor memory, they will have difficulty in following instructions, especially long or multi-step instructions, as these rely heavily on working memory. It can also affect your child's friendships because it can mean they have difficulty in tracking conversation and keeping the topic in mind. The following are further clues that your child's working memory might be impaired:

- Your child has difficulty in taking age-appropriate responsibility (e.g. remembering to feed the dog each day).

- Your child has trouble repeating back instructions to you.

- Your child has trouble in remembering lengthy instructions.

- Your child appears to forget what you've just told them.

- Your child can't seem to remember instructions long enough to follow through on a chore or activity.

- Your child can't retain the steps in a procedure once they have been read or heard.

- Your child seems to have trouble in remembering what they are meant to be doing at any given time.

We can support a child with poor working memory by adjusting our expectations to take into account their genuine difficulty in retaining information. We can help them by structuring their environment to provide visual reminders and by giving short, simple instructions. They may also benefit from games that build working memory, similar to those played by preschool children. The following strategies might help to build your child's working memory:

- Simplify their world. Use visual prompts to support your child's memory. Use simple and short sentences; this will put less demand on their working memory. Be prepared to repeat yourself.

- Incorporate reminders of all sorts into your child's day. These might be verbal reminders, sticky notes or stickers, alarms or visual reminders.

- Use categorizing and colour coding as a way to reduce demand on working memory. Categorize important information using sticky notes, different colours or pictures. For example, use a red basket for dirty clothes and a green basket for clothes that need to be put away.

- Teach your child to 'chunk' longer strings of information into bite-size chunks of two to three items or digits. This is a well-known strategy for supporting working memory.

- Chunking also helps your child to remember instructions. Break long instructions down into smaller 'bite-size' bits of information. For example, instead of saying, 'Go to your bedroom and tidy up and make sure you remember to bring down your dirty washing after you have changed' – you could try chunking this request. For example, 'Go to your room (first chunk). Get changed (second chunk). Put your washing in the red basket (third chunk). Bring your washing down to me (fourth chunk).'

- Teach your child to rehearse information, by repeating it over and over to themselves. There are many 'memory' games that can help your child practise memory 'rehearsal' (for example, 'I went to the shop and I bought...').

- Consider trying some of the commercially available programs that build attention and memory skills such as CogMed or the Amsterdam Memory training program.

Supporting the child with difficulty in flexible thinking

Being a flexible thinker means being adaptable and able to respond quickly to a changing environment. Flexible thinkers are able to alternate between different thoughts and actions, to shift easily from task to task, to come up with alternative responses to problems when frustrated and to anticipate and respond adaptively to new situations or changing circumstances and surroundings.

Flexible thinking is often impaired in children who have experienced early life adversity. Children with this kind of difficulty take more time to adapt to change of any form. These children dislike change and thrive on routine and predictability. They can get extremely anxious in anticipation of change or new and unpredictable activities, which they tend to avoid at all costs. Children who lack flexible thinking skills will find it difficult to follow changing rules and expectations. They are much more comfortable when they understand what is expected from them and what is coming up next. The following are clues that your child's flexible thinking might be impaired:

- Your child has trouble adapting to changes in routines and rituals, especially unexpected changes.

- Your child has trouble analysing a situation from another person's perspective (seeing things from another's point of view).

- Your child has difficulty in transitioning from one activity to another or transitioning between tasks or settings.

- Your child has difficulty transitioning smoothly into routines (e.g. bedtime routine).

- Your child has trouble changing strategy when something isn't working and tends to persist in the same way of doing something, despite a lack of success or despite negative feedback. For example, your child may continue with an annoying behaviour, despite feedback.

- Your child finds new or unfamiliar activities, places and people challenging.

- Your child struggles in unstructured settings such as playgrounds or in free play time.

The child with inflexible thinking will be supported by making their environment as consistent, predictable and structured as possible and by strategies to reduce their anxiety about change. You might like to try these strategies:

- Reduce novelty as much as possible and teach what you expect in new situations. Any new environment will be taxing to a child with poor flexibility.

- Teach your child the skills they need for new situations. For example, teach them how to introduce themselves to new people and get them to rehearse these skills.

- Introduce new settings and situations as gradually as possible. Highlight what is already familiar to your child (e.g. 'Jonny will be in your new class as well'). Provide your child with as much information about the impending change as possible. For example, you might provide photos of a new classroom or school.

- Always warn your child of any impending change or transition ahead of time. Wherever possible, set aside ample time for warning, supporting and explaining transitions and changes.

- Provide your child with lots of support for change and transition. Cueing and reminding can be used to warn children of impending change. This can be done using a timer, a cue such as a bell or a paper-linked chain to warn of impending change in activity (e.g. remove links in the paper chain one at a time as the time for transition draws near). Some children also find a transition object helpful (e.g. a reminder of you to take with them to new situations). It can also help to give your child an object that tells them about where they need to go and what they need to do next (e.g. bring this note to the next lesson's teacher). Ask the school to warn of substitute teachers ahead of time so your child feels prepared.

- Simplify new tasks and 'anchor' or link them to something that is familiar to your child. Aim to introduce new activities by describing how these are similar and different to activities that the child is already familiar with. New activities should be introduced by first emphasizing what is familiar (this is the same as…) before pointing out what is new or different. For example, you can say 'Jonny's house is just like our house because they have a dog and a cat. But Jonny's house is different because at Jonny's house they have a rule that you have to take off your shoes before coming inside.'

- It can also help to slow down the pace at which your child needs to think through new information. Decrease the speed, volume or complexity of any new information you give your child.

- Use forced choice questions rather than open-ended questions to provide them with a sense of control over the pace of change (e.g. 'Do you want to meet the teacher first or find your desk first?').

- Expect to provide additional support when you are introducing new tasks. New situations will require gradual and step by step assistance and reassurance. You may need to 'spell out' each new expectation and in a step by step manner (e.g. 'To clean your room, first make your bed, then pick up the toys, then pick up your washing and put it in the hamper').

- Try to involve children in planning new activities as much as possible. Anxiety about new activities, people and places can be reduced by 'habituating' your child to the event. This means introducing new activities, people or places gradually. Show your child pictures (e.g. the people that will be there, what the place looks like) so your child knows what to expect.

- Teach your child coping 'self-talk' for when 'unexpected' events occur or things don't go as planned. Practise coping self-talk ahead of time.

Supporting the child with difficulty in behavioural and emotional control

Executive control enables children to control and regulate their emotional and behavioural reactions. Children with compromised emotional and behavioural control will have disproportionate emotional and behavioural reactions.

On the one hand, children with this kind of difficulty can have extreme difficulty in inhibiting emotional and behavioural outbursts, meaning they are disinhibited in their thoughts and actions. These children have trouble in stopping themselves from voicing inappropriate thoughts and can be highly dramatic when upset. Adoptive and foster parents typically find this emotional style exhausting to manage and it commonly leads to friendship difficulties as well.

On the other hand, children with this kind of executive compromise can also have extreme difficulty in expressing emotions. These children can be extremely reserved and their emotions may seem mismatched to the situation. For example, they may not cry when hurt.

Most foster and adoptive parents are more concerned with the emotionally explosive child. We believe that children with sound emotional regulation skills and behavioural control may be less vulnerable to developing mental health concerns later in life (Morgan and Lilienfeld, 2000).

The following are clues that your child's emotional and behavioural control might be impaired:

- Your child has difficulty in recovering emotionally from minor disappointments and setbacks.

- Your child may over-react to other children's behaviour or what they say.

- Your child may have trouble controlling emotions in order to make calm decisions.

- Your child may have difficulty in self-soothing when distressed.

- Your child doesn't express emotions well (holds back excessively or lashes out).

- Your child tends to act without thinking about the consequences.

- Your child may not show distress easily, even when hurt.

If the above list describes your child, they might benefit from strategies to support their skills in emotional regulation. These typically include managing and structuring your child's social environment and teaching them strategies to reduce overall arousal levels as well as coping skills. You may like to try the following strategies:

- Try to limit your child's social interactions as much as possible to avoid specific people or situations that trigger your child's emotional or behavioural dys-regulation. If larger unstructured groups are difficult for your child to manage, consider limiting the number of friends they play with at one time.

- Provide your child with access to calming activities or toys in situations you know are difficult for them (e.g. comfort blanket). Try to pre-empt social situations in which your child typically becomes distressed.

- Teach and model soothing self-talk. Model for them how people safely express feelings when they are upset. Help them to see that feelings are normal and temporary, and that there are strategies that we can use to calm ourselves and express emotions safely.

- Children who are emotionally inhibited can be supported to build their emotional literacy using the strategies in Chapter 6.

- Children who are emotionally explosive may also benefit from strategies to build their emotional literacy (see Chapter 6). Many emotionally explosive children are comfortable with negative emotions (such as anger); however, they may have very few words for positive emotions.

- Look for everyday opportunities to teach your child emotional cues and how to recognize feelings in others.

- Empathize with your child's emotions – reflect back to them how they are feeling. Help them to name the emotion they are experiencing. Take their emotion seriously (even if it seems overly dramatic). Providing empathy is not the same as condoning the behaviour; you're just letting your child know that you understand the emotion behind the behaviour. Showing a genuine interest in the emotional state of your child will help them to recognize the importance of feelings that might not have been valued in their family of origin.

- Teach your child the limits of appropriate emotional expression (when, where and with whom it is safe to share emotions). Help them identify who they can safely confide in, and who to go to if they are upset outside the home.

- Help your child to develop coping and 'cool off' strategies that they can use when overwhelmed. Practise setting limits but don't expect your child to manage strong emotions themselves initially.

- Teach and practise relaxation strategies. Relaxation and mindfulness strategies 'turn down' the thermostat on your child's arousal level, give them the skills for self-calming under pressure and help them to develop body–mind awareness. There are many brief mindfulness and relaxation techniques for children available on the internet (e.g. the 'turtle technique').

Chapter 8

Developmental Difference in Social Information Processing

In this chapter, we'll look at the last area of developmental difference in children who have experienced early life adversity. We now believe that these children may process the social world in a different way and one that leads to difficulty in forming social relationships: namely altered social information processing. This developmental difference appears to take one of two forms: enhanced attention to threats in the social environment or a reduced enjoyment of social interactions.

Researchers have understood for a while now that there is a link between early childhood adversity and risk for mental health difficulties later in life, but they haven't really understood how these two things are connected.

In recent times researchers have begun to build up a picture of the way that a brain responds to the social world (this is called social information processing) and how these brain responses are affected by early life adversity and trauma. Using this approach, researchers have been able to detect some differences in the way that that people who have experienced early life adversity process social information.

These studies, called functional brain imaging studies, have explored how the brain reacts to the social world in 'real time'– as it happens – helping us to develop an accurate picture of the cognitive processes that underlie children's reaction to their social world and what children's experience of the social world might be. These studies have also provided us with an insight into how these developmental differences in social processing *could* increase a child's vulnerability to developing mental health issues later in life. This is an emerging area of research and much work remains to be done to build up the evidence base, so the issues discussed in this chapter are based on early and tentative findings in this field (see the resources section at the end of the book for research details if you are interested in finding out more).

This chapter summarizes two aspects of suggested developmental difference in how children respond and interact with their social world. Although the evidence is suggestive, rather than clear cut, these differences do align with what many adoptive and foster parents already know. That is, that some children can find social relationships unrewarding and anxiety-laden experiences. In this chapter, we'll look at two of the ways that children's social development can differ as a result of early experiences. Emerging research suggests that affected children:

- may show an *enhanced threat response* in social situations and social interactions (suggesting they find social interactions more threatening, fearful and anxiety laden), and

- may show reduced triggering of *brain reward* pathways in social situations and social interactions (suggesting they don't find social interactions rewarding).

These differences are thought to be automatic – occurring below the level of consciousness – and are not within a child's control. This chapter will explore the main implications of this emerging research for supporting children. Much of the information here comes from our developing knowledge about positive psychology approaches and mindfulness training on children's well-being. We believe there is lot we can do to support children who might experience developmental differences in social processing. Before moving onto strategies, let's look at these two developmental differences in social processing and what these mean for children.

Enhanced sense of social threat

The brains of children exposed to early adversity may be biased towards triggering a threat response to everyday social events and social stimuli. Everyday social situations may trigger an automatic 'threat' response to social events that others don't find threatening.

In earlier times (earlier in our evolution) the ability to rapidly detect and react to threat gave us a great advantage over predators. This instantaneous, automatic and powerful 'threat detection' pathway in our brains triggers the 'fight or flight' survival responses (McCrory, Gerin and Viding, 2017; Öhman et al., 2007; Öhman, 2009) and has been critical to our survival during adversity.

For children who have not experienced adversity, this pathway is only activated in times of extreme fear or trauma (for example, if a child is attacked by a dog). For children who have experienced adversity and trauma, however, there appears to be a 'mis-cueing' of this response; it becomes so 'over-efficient' in reacting to threat, that even events that aren't actually dangerous are able to trigger this response. As a result, we believe children may consistently respond to both threatening and benign everyday social interactions as though they were dangerous.

We think this happens because a child's early experience has been that people are dangerous and frightening. It may be more likely in children that have experienced inconsistent and frightening caregiving and neglect. This experience causes the innate fear response to become powerfully linked to 'being with people'. This is involuntary and automatic; it occurs at a neural response level (we are not conscious of it) and involves heightened and persistent brain reactivity to both neutral and 'dangerous' emotional stimuli (McCrory et al., 2017). We believe that this developmental difference could lay the neural foundation for the development of anxiety disorders in later life by creating social avoidance behaviour in young people. This is significant, because avoidance of perceived (not actual) danger plays a central role in developing anxiety disorders.

An anxious child consistently feels that feared events, situations or objects are more threatening than they actually are. A child with persistent threat response may be more likely to develop an anxiety disorder over time because the *perception of threat* is central to the development of anxiety. For these reasons, it is important to acknowledge children's fears, and build children's coping and resilience in the face of anxiety. We think that the following principles are helpful for children who may be prone to developing anxiety:

- Make sure to create a safe and predictable home environment for your child. This might sound obvious, but it is a critical first step towards dampening a child's threat response. When children experience psychological safety, it reduces the need for them to constantly scan their world for potential threats. A structured and predictable home life, with consistent care from reliable and responsive adults, can help to foster feelings of safety (Kinniburgh *et al.*, 2005).

- Educate your child about threat bias and anxiety. It is helpful to give your child an age-appropriate explanation for their feelings (Donker *et al.*, 2009). Explain to children how their clever brains have helped them by becoming 'wired' to be threat detectors and that this was a clever way for them to survive a difficult family life. It can be really powerful to acknowledge the importance of this strategy for your child. There are many websites that explain to children how their clever brains and their 'threat bias' have helped them to survive trauma.

- Educate yourself about how to support a child that might be prone to social anxiety. Several websites offer free educational materials for caregivers regarding anxiety and avoidance. The Children's Anxiety Institute has free resources developed by caregivers for caregivers of children with anxiety. The Child Mind Institute has information about how cognitive behavioural approaches may benefit children who are prone to anxiety. This information is included in the resources section for this chapter.

Children who are already experiencing mild anxiety may be supported by applying the following evidence-based principles, which may be delivered in conjunction with a psychologist:

- *Practise relaxation training:* Children preschool age and older can benefit from relaxation training, especially where children have developed anxiety that is accompanied by physical symptoms (stomach ache, nausea, etc.). There are several forms of relaxation training for children, including progressive muscle relaxation, guided breathing techniques, guided imagery, mindful visualization and cued relaxation. It is important to check with children if you are intending to use imagery or physical touch with children in case there is an association with past trauma. Relaxation techniques lower overall arousal and can be used as coping strategies when feeling unsafe. I've included links to example relaxation scripts in the resources section for this chapter (Inner Health Studio and Therapist Aid).

- *Teach children to be thought 'detectives':* School-aged children who are prone to anxiety can also benefit from learning 'thought challenging' exercises. These can be delivered in conjunction with a psychologist. The core experience of anxiety involves the child's magnifying potential threat in their mind. Anxiety is also commonly associated with distorted thinking or 'thinking styles'. When children use these thinking styles it fuels their perception that the world is a dangerous place. In 'thought detective' exercises, children are taught to identify these unhelpful thinking styles and to weigh up the evidence for, and against, these thought distortions (this is the basis for cognitive behaviour therapy). Anxious children often engage in 'fortune telling', 'over-generalization' and 'catastrophizing' (Muris and Field, 2008). See Box 10 for a description of unhelpful thinking styles that are associated with risk of anxiety and depression.

- *Make a plan to overcome avoidance:* The child's avoidance of potential anxiety-provoking situations also contributes to anxiety disorders. Avoidance behaviour reinforces the idea that situations are dangerous or threatening. Avoidance is typically managed by developing a plan for gradually exposing a child to a feared event or activity. This is done in consultation with the child and a psychologist who helps develop their 'ladder' of feared situations. In this approach, situations that are perceived as fearful are tackled one by one, from least to most threatening. The 'ladder' approach allows a child to experience and tolerate feared activities beginning with less anxiety-provoking situations and building up to more feared events. For example, a socially anxious child might start with saying hello to a child they know, and progress in increments to introducing themselves to unknown children. Each step of the 'ladder' involves progressing to slightly more difficult tasks, and before each task is attempted, the child practises coping and tolerance skills. This gives them a safe experience of successfully coping with feared situations, building their confidence over time. Referral to a psychologist is indicated when a child has longstanding avoidance or when their fears are so generalized and extensive that they impact on their participation in school and community activities. A link to the ladder approach (Raising Children Network) is included in the resources section for this chapter.

- *Help your child to learn to tolerate distress:* Children who are prone to anxiety often believe that the experience of anxiety is intolerable (this belief is often associated with early life experiences in which fear was indeed overwhelming). For this reason, an important part of supporting an anxiety-prone child will often be to include activities that gradually increase a child's 'window of tolerance' for distress. The aim is that your child learns that, by using coping skills and relaxation, they will be able to tolerate feelings of anxiety and have the skills to manage these feelings. I've included some websites about this in the resource section of this chapter.

Diminished sense of social reward

The other area of social difference in children exposed to early life adversity appears to be a diminished sense of reward in social situations. These children may not get the same enjoyment from social events or activities as their non-abused peers because these activities are not perceived or processed in the same way. Although we don't know for sure, we believe that this developmental difference in the experience of social reward could lay the neural foundation for the development of depression and addiction in adolescence and later life (McCrory et al., 2017; McLean, 2018a, 2018b).

Brain researchers believe that there are several reward pathways in our brains. These pathways are involved in making us feel good when we are engaged in social behaviour. We learn to enjoy social interactions because these activities trigger the 'feel good' hormones in the brain. This kind of 'feel good' biochemistry in the brain is designed to strengthen and reinforce social connection to others and is part of what makes social relationships so rewarding. However, these social reward pathways appear to be less 'active' in some maltreated children and adults. Their response to social reward is diminished (McCrory, et al., 2017), meaning they may find social interaction unrewarding. We believe that this diminished experience of 'reward' in social interactions may convey a vulnerability to depression in later life.

For children affected in this way, it is important to try to help them to 'recalibrate' their social reward systems. We need to build their resilience and capacity for experiencing social pleasure (see *Cognitive Therapy with Children and Adolescents: A Casebook for Clinical Practice* by Reinecke, Dattilio and Freeman, 2003). We think that the following principles are helpful for children who may be less responsive to the rewarding aspects of social interaction:

- *Provide your child with an age-appropriate explanation for their experiences:* Explain to your child how their brain has helped them by 'learning not to expect good feelings' and that this was a clever way to survive difficult circumstances. It can be important to acknowledge the past value of this strategy; this can give your child a more positive self-identity and a more optimistic outlook on their future.

- *Teach your child to be a thought 'detective':* Do this in conjunction with a psychologist, for the reasons outlined earlier in this chapter. Children can come to magnify the negative aspects of a social interaction and minimize the positive aspects. These automatic patterns of thinking fuel the perception that social relationships are unrewarding, leading to a vicious cycle of social avoidance. Children can be taught to act as 'thought detectives', weighing up the evidence for their perception of a situation. A psychologist is trained to teach children to identify these kinds of unhelpful thinking styles and provide structured 'thought challenging' exercises to reduce these thinking styles over time (see Box 10 for the common thinking styles associated with depression and anxiety). These automatic thinking styles fuel children's innate perception that social relationships are unrewarding.

- *Use activity scheduling:* It can be helpful to make a habit of scheduling regular social activities. Start with very brief activities that your child finds enjoyable and build up to more prolonged social experiences. Your child may need relatively brief and structured social interactions to begin with. It is likely to take regular practice and time to overcome a child's social reluctance.

- *Use positive psychology strategies:* If your child is old enough, it can be helpful to help them develop the habit of paying attention to positive aspects of their social relationships. One example of this is keeping a gratitude journal (using words or pictures), whereby young people are encouraged to notice and record positive aspects of their daily social interactions (Froh *et al.*, 2014). Journalling should focus on 'noticing' the rewarding aspects of relationships and on identifying and documenting experiences of feeling safe in social situations (even if this feeling was fleeting). Other positive psychology strategies, such as practising acts of kindness and mindfulness skills, can also be helpful (Seligman *et al.*, 2009; Weare and Hind, 2011).

There is also some new and emerging research to suggest the potential benefit of some of the mental health apps that are now available for mobile phones or tablets (Bakker *et al.*, 2016). These offer a portable means for accessing low cost, easy to follow exercises and activities designed to build resiliency. Available research suggest that apps that use a combination of attention training, thought challenging and set homework activities are most effective (Bakker *et al.*, 2016). Attention training involves training the child to attend more to positive (social) stimuli and less to adverse stimuli, through highly repetitive screen activities. Behavioural activation involves scheduling activities that involve real life exposure and opportunities to practise coping skills.

When to seek professional support

The information in this chapter is not intended for children with moderate or severe depression or anxiety. It provides preventative strategies that can support children who may otherwise be vulnerable to depression and anxiety later in life. If you are concerned that a child has developed anxiety that is persistent and interferes with their capacity for participating in daily activities, you will need to arrange for them to access a cognitive behavioural treatment plan, delivered by a trained professional. Similarly, you should be concerned if your child's behaviour or mood has changed, if your child is more withdrawn than usual, shows less interest in activities and events they previously enjoyed, shows changes in their sleep or eating habits, or talks about suicide or self-harm. In this case, urgent assessment and professional support is needed (Kangas, 2014). Typically, children can be referred to a general practitioner, who can determine if the child should be referred to a psychologist. If this is not feasible, then it is also possible in most cases to take your child to a children's hospital for assessment.

When in doubt, seek help

If you are concerned that your child is more withdrawn than usual, shows less interest in activities they previously enjoyed or shows changes in sleep or appetite, then arrange an appointment with a doctor who can organize a referral to a psychologist or psychiatrist for a mental health assessment. If your child's social reluctance is limiting their access to social and community activities, you should seek professional support. You can also call or visit the local children's hospital for an urgent mental health assessment.

BOX 10

Common thinking styles associated with risk of depression or anxiety

Below are some of the unhelpful thinking styles that can be associated with the development of depression or anxiety. A psychologist is trained in identifying and addressing these thinking styles.

- *Black and white thinking:* Sometimes called 'all or nothing thinking', this involves always only seeing one extreme or another (for example, seeing something as 'all bad' or 'all good'); in black and white thinking there are no 'shades of grey'.

- *Catastrophizing:* This thinking style involves 'blowing things out of proportion' and imagining that events are terrible, disastrous or irreversible, when in reality even in the 'worst-case' scenario, the impact would be minimal.

- *Filtering:* This thinking style is like having 'tunnel vision', excessively focusing on the negative aspects of a situation, and dismissing or not noticing the positive aspects of that situation.

- *Fortune telling:* Fortune telling occurs when we automatically make predictions about what will happen in the future, typically based on an imagined 'worst-case scenario', rather than being based on facts.

- *Labelling:* We use labelling when we make global judgements about ourselves that are based on specific situations but become entrenched beliefs about ourselves (e.g. 'I'm stupid', rather than 'I made a stupid mistake'). In this thinking style, these 'labels' persist in our minds, despite multiple examples that contradict our self-labels.

- *Over-generalization:* This thinking style involves taking one event from the past and imposing it on all current or future situations. This is often signalled by a child saying 'You always...', or 'I never...'.

- *'Shoulding' and 'musting':* This thinking style occurs when we put unreasonable demands on ourselves by thinking 'I should...do/say/ be' or 'I must...'. By using these statements we often create unrealistic demands on ourselves.

Chapter 9

Communicating About Your Child's Developmental Difference to Others

In this chapter, we'll look at potential strategies for communicating with the busy professionals in your child's life. As an adoptive or foster parent, you are likely to be liaising with many different professionals and coordinating multiple services so that you can get the necessary support for your child. There is no doubt that this can be a frustrating experience for many adoptive and foster parents.

One of the most important relationships you will have is the one you have with your child's social worker. When this relationship is strong, you'll feel supported and understood. When this relationship is strained, it may become difficult to get the support your child needs. This chapter provides tips from carers that you may find useful in working with your child's social worker. Although the focus is on communicating and negotiating with social workers, these principles are applicable to other key professionals as well (e.g. teachers).

Potential barriers to communicating with your child's social worker

Child protection social workers face many stressors in their work. Although they are trained professionals, these stressors can erode their sense of achievement, well-being and effectiveness over time. Child protection social work is also very complex work. A child protection social worker often needs to make decisions that draw on broader understandings of child development, collaborative and respectful decision making, child protection policies and procedures, and 'best interests' principles. This kind of knowledge is gained over time and with experience. Many workers may not yet have had the opportunity to develop this knowledge. It's useful to keep this in mind when talking to your child's social worker. So before we move onto strategies to advocate for your child, let's take some time to consider the main barriers that can affect a worker's ability to work in partnership with you.

Workload

Child protection case workers can be overworked and burdened with caseloads that prevent them really getting to know the children for whom they are responsible. This is often in stark contrast to what they would like to do; most child protection workers really want to have a personal relationship with the children under their care. Although in most countries, a child's social worker is supposed to visit regularly, they may not actually have this capacity.

Workload pressures also mean that they need to prioritize children who are experiencing a crisis over those that are placed in a safe home. Once a child is placed, there can be a pressure to move onto finding a home for the next child.

Workload pressures also mean that workers rarely have time to take on additional tasks that aren't critical to what they need to accomplish that day. It can be helpful to keep your emails brief and ensure they contain a brief 'positive news story'. This keeps your child's caseworker up to date, but also builds their confidence in you. While this may seem like a lot of effort and all 'give and no take', carers report it is a good way to foster a positive relationship with a busy caseworker. This may mean that you are more likely to get prompt and positive response when needed.

Emotional availability

This pressured work environment can also mean that your worker is less emotionally available and empathic when you want to raise issues with them. Although social workers are highly skilled in engaging with and understanding others, the pressures of the work culture may not give them opportunity to use these skills.

The child protection workforce is an action-oriented workplace; your child's caseworker works in a high pressure environment that values 'deciding and doing'. Child protection social workers are expected to take action and solve problems as they arise. This may mean that when you call them, they are thinking about what they will need to do in response to your call. Phone conversations may be viewed as you bringing problems to be solved, rather than as you looking for someone to discuss your child's needs with. If possible, see if you can organize a specific time to talk to your child's worker, rather than catching them 'on the run'. This may help to create a safe space and time for communicating about your child.

Experience of parenting

Some child protection workers also have little personal experience of parenting. This can mean that it may not be as easy for them to understand your perspective on issues. A worker may not automatically consider the impact on your household and other children. They may need you to highlight to them how the timing of appointments or family access visits affects your home and family.

Knowledge of child development

Some caseworkers may have little experience of distinguishing between 'normal' and concerning child behaviours. This can sometimes mean that your concerns are unintentionally minimized or even dismissed. You could be seen as exaggerating your child's support needs. In the worst case, your concerns may be seen as an indication that you aren't coping, that you are not a skilled parent or that the placement is a poor 'match'. For this reason, ensure you have clear 'data' and facts to present to your child's caseworker. Try to keep conversations about your child's behaviour and support needs as 'matter of fact' as possible whenever you can.

Authority

Ultimately, your child's social worker may not even have the mandate to authorize decisions that have financial implications for the child protection department. A worker may need to 'make a case' to their supervisor. Having a good record and clear 'data' from you will also help your worker to advocate for your child with their supervisor in a 'matter-of-fact' and un-emotional way.

Communicating effectively with your child's social worker

In light of all the pressures outlined above, it is important to be as prepared as possible in terms of *what* and *how* you communicate with your child's social worker. You may find it useful to follow the principles below. (I've also provided an example conversation plan that may help you to have difficult conversations.)

Determine the purpose of your conversation

Remind yourself of the purpose of the conversation you are having. Keep in mind the goal of the conversation and the outcome you are seeking. This will help you to avoid getting drawn off topic if things get emotional. This is particularly important in 'high stakes' conversations – when the outcome is important. Remind yourself of what you hope to achieve from the conversation. Is it understanding? Or are you seeking approval for specialist support? Do you want approval for a particular activity or travel? Take time to write down your goal, and what you will accept as an alternative. Stay focused on what you want to achieve for your child.

Prepare what you want to say and how you want to say it. Adoptive and foster parents also suggest that it is most effective to focus on one issue at a time. Focus your energy on the issue that will make the most impact on your child's life and set the others aside for the moment. In your conversation, it is helpful to show that you have thought about possible solutions and are happy to enact these. Research options and present these to your child's caseworker as *possible* solutions to accessing supports. You may be viewed as more cooperative if you are flexible with the solutions on offer, unless there is a very good reason not to be. In other words, your goal should be clear, but be prepared to go to 'plan B' if needed. Be clear about what outcome is desirable, and what outcome is acceptable.

Consider the way you communicate

Being mindful of the *way* you communicate is more difficult. It is very easy to get emotional or defensive when advocating for your child with caseworkers who don't seem to understand. Needless to say, this is not necessarily the most effective approach. Instead, try to do the following:

- Stay calm, professional and positive.

- Resist the urge to get drawn into negative interactions.

- Stay focused on working on the problem, rather than responding to emotions, implied criticisms and blaming.

- Respond to their feelings, or how you imagine they must be feeling.

- Don't interrupt.

- Stay focused on evidence, rather than arguing about the interpretation.

Collect all relevant information: prepare

Determine exactly what it is that you want to communicate about. Are you talking about an isolated event? Or about a pattern of related events? The nature and severity of the behaviour will determine how you frame the conversation, and what kind of response you are seeking. It can be helpful to write down your goal – what is it you want from this conversation?

Gather together the information you need to advocate for your child. This might include a summary of any specialist reports, your observations, your diary notes, what you have learned from completing behaviour checklists or what your child tells you is going on for them.

Try to make your information as objective as possible. Wherever possible note whether the issue has been happening for a long time (e.g. on previous placements) or has only begun recently. Don't assume that the caseworker you talk to will be familiar with your child's history. Caseworkers may have very little time to read children's files, which can be lengthy. You can really help shape the direction of the conversation if you are able to provide a good summary of what you know and have observed. Having your information summarized and at your fingertips will be useful in advocating effectively for your child.

Talk to other adoptive and foster carers: seek advice

Do you know someone who has been successful in getting their child's needs addressed? Perhaps another foster or adoptive parent? Ask them for advice. How did they do it? What advice do they have for you? What do they know about available resources and how to access these? Are there any specialists or schools that are better than others? What do they know about which workers are more effective? Talking to other carers can help you to formulate a clear plan about what you want for your child – which specialist, which school, which programme and so on. Gather information about potential costs and waiting lists. Assess this information yourself as your worker is unlikely to have the time to do this. Having a clear plan that draws on local carer knowledge and experience will help overcome the kinds of barriers described above. Experienced carers can be your most valuable source of information in preparing to negotiate for your child.

Take a moment to see things from the worker's point of view

Prior to making that call, take a moment to see things from your worker's point of view.

- What kind of pressures is your child's caseworker likely to experience?

- Does this social worker actually know your child or are they new to your child's life?

- What story are they likely to have about this child?

- Why do you think the support you are requesting hasn't been provided earlier? (Does their supervisor agree that extra support is needed or not? Are there other issues to be resolved before they agree to specialist support?)

Ask yourself how you can make it easier for a caseworker to support your child:

- Is it better to provide a written summary of your observations so the worker can take these to their supervisor?

- Would it help to research a range of options and present these as well?

- How can you ensure that you remain calm and objective?

- How might a caseworker interpret your behaviour if you get angry or upset?

- What message do you want to send this worker about your role in this child's life?

Before starting a difficult conversation check if there is time to have this conversation. Trying to have a difficult conversation when the timing isn't right for either party is a recipe for disaster. If possible, organize a set time to have a meeting or phone call. Before starting, ask the caseworker if this is still a good time to have a conversation. Gaining this permission from your child's worker commits them to setting aside this time and conveys the message that this is an important conversation.

Consider using a script to guide your conversation

If you anticipate a difficult conversation, it can be useful to prepare a plan. A conversation plan can help you to stay focused on what is most relevant. Here's an example of what a conversation could look like; but you can create your own, using your own language. It is important to keep the emphasis on a clear problem statement and on remaining focused on the child's needs, along the lines of the script below:

STATE THE PROBLEM CLEARLY

Here are some examples of how you might clearly state the issue that needs to be discussed. The key is to bring the focus clearly on your child's needs:

'I'd like to talk to you about _____ (my child).'

'I'm really committed to providing a stable home for _____ (my child). I want to discuss something that will help me to do that.'

'I've notice something that concerns me and I'd like to tell you what I've noticed.'

'I've noticed that _____ (my child) has trouble
with _____ in the following situations
_____ (when, where and how often).'

EXPLAIN THE IMPACT ON YOUR CHILD'S LIFE

Try to convey the broader impact of your child's difficulty on their
life. Let your child's worker know that the issue impacts on more
than just you and your family life. This helps 'de-personalize' the
discussion and refocus it on how your child's life is affected. Here
are some examples statements you could use:

'I've wondered if this is something that only happens at home
with us, but I've noticed this is also something that happens
in other places, for example _____.'

'I've wondered if this is something that only affects me, but
_____ (others) have also noticed this.'

'This difficulty means _____ (my child) is not able to
_____ (attend school/join in activities/
sleep at night/play well with friends).'

'I've wondered if this is something that has only happened since
he/she has been living with us. I've talked to _____
(my child) and he/she tells me this was something he/she also
struggled with in his/her last home.'

OFFER POSSIBLE SOLUTIONS TO THE DIFFICULTY

It is important to bring potential solutions to your worker. Try
not to be attached to any one solution. Present plan A, but be
prepared to accept plan B. This enables your child's worker to
have a sense of control over decisions. Try to remain 'solution'
focused, not problem focused.

'I've looked at a few child development checklists and this
seems to show that _____ (my child) needs help
with _____ (e.g. sensory
issues, organization skills, language and communication). Can
I share this information with you?'

'I've found some strategies and resources that can be useful. Most resources suggest that a specialist _____ assessment can help in this situation.'

'I've made a summary of this information that I can send to you.'

'I'm really committed to supporting my child and to providing him/her with the best opportunities that I can in life. I'd really like your support with that.'

'I've found the name of someone in my area that can help and I was wondering if we can talk about getting a referral? These are the details of the cost...'.

STAY FOCUSED ON YOUR CHILD'S NEEDS

No matter where the conversation leads, it is important to keep returning the conversation to your child's needs. Assume that your child's worker has your child's best interests at heart and convey that belief to the worker. Adopt a 'we' attitude to moving forward towards a good outcome for your child. Some example statements might include the following:

'I know we are both interested in providing the best possible support for _____ (child). I hope that we can work together to make sure that this happens.'

'What is the likely cost to this child if we are not able to work together to get him/her the supports he/she needs?'

DON'T GIVE UP WHEN YOU GET A 'NO'

Don't give up when you get a 'no' initially. Remain focused on the child's needs, gather more information and try again. Remember to stay calm despite the frustration. Try to empathize with the caseworker and the difficult work that they do. At the same time, don't let your social worker's workload pressures deter you from your request. Instead of accepting a 'no', it can be useful to ask about ways forward. For example:

'What do you think is keeping us from reaching an agreement about my child's needs?'

'What more information do you need from me to feel confident about supporting my request?'

'What would you or your supervisor need to feel more comfortable about agreeing to my request?'

'How long will it be before we can talk again about this issue?'

'What information can I give you in the meantime?'

Chapter 10

Summary

We've seen that children who have experienced early adversity of all kinds are likely to experience a range of developmental differences that can have significant implications for their life. These developmental differences also have significant implications for the way you support your child.

It's important to start by asking 'What's different for my child?' rather than 'What's wrong with my child?' This mindset allows you to start thinking in terms of the environmental modifications, skills and supports that your child needs to address their developmental difference.

Throughout this book, we've looked at three main ways that children with developmental difference can be supported. We can think of these principles as sound preventative strategies for children with developmental difference. It is important to re-visit these principles from time to time, and especially when things get wobbly. Let's re-visit these now.

Re-evaluate your expectations

When things get tricky stop and consider if you need to adjust your expectations of your child. Are you expecting more from them than they are currently capable of? What do you need to do differently to better meet their needs? How can you meet your child at their current developmental level? Shifting your mindset to thinking in terms of your child's developmental difference really takes the pressure off your child. Remind yourself it's not that your child *won't* do what you ask; it's that they *can't*.

Modify your child's environment

Ask yourself what you can do to make the world less taxing for your child. How can you make it easier for your child to be successful? Simplify, structure and supervise – make it easier for your child to experience success. In each chapter we provided you with some ideas for how to go about this. Common strategies for simplifying your child's environment include making their world more predictable and structured, using visual prompts and simplifying your child's social interactions. Simplifying the environment takes the pressure off your child and helps them to manage everyday situations that might otherwise overwhelm them.

Build your child's competence

Ask yourself what your child needs to be able to do differently. What coping skills does your child need? What do they not know that they need to know? What skills might be delayed? So much of what we do every day relies on skills that are learned early in life and in an effortless way. You can foster your child's development when you are able to 'plug the gap' in their knowledge by teaching them, through a variety of ways, the skills they need to succeed. It is only when children feel competent and have a strategy for managing their frustrations that they will be comfortable enough to relinquish their challenging behaviour. These skills often include the ability to tolerate strong emotions; the skills of self-regulation of feelings and sensory sensitivities; skills of memory and organization; and language and communication skills.

Finally

I hope this book has given you a sense of how your child might experience the world and about how you might support your child's development in the context of their unique differences. For more information about supporting children with developmental difference, visit the Fostering Difference website where you will find resources for both carers and social workers.

About the Author

Dr Sara McLean is a Consultant Psychologist in Child Protection and past recipient of the ACU Linacre Fellowship at the Rees Centre for Research on Fostering and Education, Oxford University; and an Adjunct Research Fellow at the Australian Centre for Child Protection, University of South Australia. She has written extensively about the support needs of foster parents and children in care. She is also the author of the Fostering Difference website, and associated training and support materials.

Resources

Chapter 1

Anda, R.F., Felitti, V.J. and Bremner, J.D. (2006). The enduring effects of abuse and related adverse experiences in childhood: A convergence of evidence from neurobiology and epidemiology. *European Archives of Psychiatry and Clinical Neuroscience 256*, 174–186.

Atkinson, J. (2013). *Trauma-Informed Services and Trauma-Specific Care for Indigenous Australian Children* (Closing the Gap Clearinghouse Resource 21). Canberra: Australian Institute of Health and Welfare.

Carrion, V.G., Weems, C.F., Richert, K., Hoffman, B.C. and Reiss, A.L. (2010). Decreased prefrontal cortical volume associated with increased bedtime cortisol in traumatized youth. *Biological Psychiatry 68*, 5, 491–493.doi. org/10.1016/j.biopsych.2010.05.010

Cascio, C. (2010). Somatosensory processing in neurodevelopmental disorders. *Journal of Neurodevelopmental Disorders 2*, 9046. doi.org/10.1007/s11689-010-9046-3

Cermak, S. and Groza, V. (1998). Sensory processing problems in post-institutionalized children: Implications for social work. *Child and Adolescent Social Work Journal 15*, 5. doi.org/10.1023/A:1022241403962

Cicchetti, D., Rogosch, F.A., Gunnar, M.R. and Toth, S.L. (2010). The differential impacts of early physical and sexual abuse and internalizing problems on daytime cortisol rhythm in school-aged children. *Child Development 81*, 252–269.

Cook, A., Spinazzola, J., Ford, J.D., Lanktree, C., Blaustein, M. Cloitre, M *et al.* (2005). Complex trauma in children and adolescents. *Psychiatric Annals 35*, 5, 390–398.

De Bellis, M.D., Keshavan, M.S., Shifflett, H., Iyengar, S., Beers, S., Hall, J. *et al.* (2002). Brain structures in pediatric maltreatment-related posttraumatic stress disorder: A sociodemographically matched study. *Biological Psychiatry 52*, 1066–1078.

De Bellis, M.D., Hooper, S.R., Spratt, E.G. and Woolley, D.P. (2009). Neuropsychological findings in childhood neglect and their relationships to pediatric PTSD. *Journal of the International Neuropsychological Society 15*, 868–878.

De Brito, S.A., Viding, E., Sebastian, C.L., Kelly, P.A., Mechelli, A., Maris, H. and McCrory, E.J. (2013). Reduced orbitofrontal and temporal gray matter in a community sample of maltreated children. *The Journal of Child Psychology and Psychiatry 54*, 105–112. [PubMed: 22880630]

De Jong, M. (2010). Some reflections on the use of psychiatric diagnosis in the looked after or 'in care' child population. *Clinical Child Psychology and Psychiatry 15*, 4, 589–599.

De Lisi, M. and Vaughn, M.G. (2011). The importance of neuropsychological deficits relating to self-control and temperament to the prevention of serious antisocial behaviour. *International Journal of Child, Youth and Family Studies 1 and 2*, 12–35.

DePrince, A.P., Weinzierl, K.M. and Combs, M.D. (2009). Executive function performance and trauma exposure in a community sample of children. *Child Abuse and Neglect 33*, 353–361. [PubMed: 19477515]

Dvir, Y., Ford, J.D., Hill, M. and Frazier, J.A. (2014). Childhood maltreatment, emotional dysregulation, and psychiatric comorbidities. *Harvard Review of Psychiatry 22*, 3, 149–161. doi:10.1097/HRP.0000000000000014

Emerson, E. (1995). *Challenging Behaviour: Analysis and Intervention in People with Learning Disabilities.* Cambridge: Cambridge University Press.

Ford, T., Vostanis, P., Meltzer, H. and Goodman, R. (2007). Psychiatric disorder among British children looked after by local authorities: Comparison with children living in private households. *British Journal of Psychiatry 190*, 319–325. doi.org/10.1192/bjp.bp.106.025023

Franklin, L., Deitz, J., Jirikowic, T. and Astley, S. (2008). Children with fetal alcohol spectrum disorders: Problem behaviors and sensory processing. *American Journal of Occupational Therapy 62*, 265–273.

Frodl, T. and O'Keane, V. (2013). How does the brain deal with cumulative stress? A review with focus on developmental stress, HPA axis function and hippocampal structure in humans. *Neurobiology of Disease 52*, 24–37.

Grant, K. and Gravestock, F. (2003). Speech and language impairment: A neglected issue for abused and neglected children. *Children Australia 28*, 4, 4–11.

Hart, H. and Rubia, K. (2012). Neuroimaging of child abuse: A critical review. *Frontiers in Human Neuroscience 6*, 52.

Hildyard K.L. and Wolfe, D.A. (2002). Child neglect: Developmental issues and outcomes. *Child Abuse and Neglect 26*, 679–695. [PubMed: 12201162]

Kelly, P.A., Viding, E., Wallace, G.L., Schaer, M. *et al.* (2013). Cortical thickness, surface area, and gyrification abnormalities in children exposed to maltreatment: Neural markers of vulnerability? *Biological Psychiatry 74*, 845–852. [PubMed: 23954109]

Koenen, K., Moffitt, T.E., Caspi, A., Taylor, A. and Purcell, S. (2003). Domestic violence is associated with environmental suppression of IQ in young children. *Development and Psychopathology 15*, 297–315.

Kuo, J.R., Khoury, J.E., Metcalfe, R., Fitzpatrick, S. and Goodwill, A. (2015). An examination of the relationship between childhood emotional abuse and borderline personality disorder features: The role of difficulties with emotional regulation. *Child Abuse and Neglect 39*, 147–155. doi.org/10.1016/j.chiabu.2014.08.008

Lansdown, R., Burnell, A. and Allen, M. (2007). Is it that they won't do it, or is it that they can't? Executive functioning and children who have been fostered and adopted. *Adoption and Fostering 31*, 2, 44–53.

Luke, N., Sinclair, I., Woolgar, M. and Sebba, J. (2014). What works in preventing and treating poor mental health in looked after children? NSPCC and Oxford University. Accessed on 6/6/2018 at www.nspcc.org.uk/globalassets/documents/evaluation-of-services/preventing-treating-mental-health-looked-after-children-summary

McCrory, E.J., De Brito, S.A., Sebastian, C.L., Mechelli, A. *et al.* (2011). Heightened neural reactivity to threat in child victims of family violence. *Current Biology 21*, R947–R948. [PubMed: 22153160]

McCrory, E., De Brito, S.A. and Viding, E. (2010). Research review: The neurobiology and genetics of maltreatment and adversity. *Journal Child Psychology and Psychiatry 51*, 1079–1095.

McCrory, E., Gerin, M.L. and Viding, E. (2017). Annual Research Review: Childhood maltreatment, latent vulnerability and the shift to preventative psychiatry – the contribution of functional brain imaging. *The Journal of Child Psychology and Psychiatry 58*, 4, 338–357.

McEwen, B.S. (2012). Brain on stress: How the social environment gets under the skin. *Proceedings of the National Academy of Sciences 109*, 17180–17185. [PubMed: 20840167]

McLaughlin, K.A., Sheridan, M.A. and Lambert, H.K. (2014). Childhood adversity and neural development: Deprivation and threat as distinct dimensions of early experience. *Neuroscience and Biobehavioural Review 47*, 578–591. doi:10.1016/j.neubiorev.2014.10.012

McLean, S. (2016a). Children's attachment needs in the context of out of home care. CFCA Practitioner Resource, November 2016. Accessed on 6/6/2018 at aifs.gov.au/cfca/publications/childrens-attachment-needs-context-out-home-care

McLean, S. (2016b). The effect of trauma on the brain development of children: Evidence-based principles for supporting the recovery of children in care. Accessed on 6/6/2018 at aifs.gov.au/cfca/publications/effect-trauma-brain-development-children

McLean, S. and McDougall, S. (2014). Fetal alcohol spectrum disorders: Current issues in awareness, prevention and intervention. CFCA Paper 29. Melbourne: Australian Institute for Family Studies.

McLean, S., McDougall, S. and Russell, V. (2014). Supporting children living with FASD: Practice principles. CFCA Practicitioner Resource. Melbourne: Australian Institute for Family Studies.

Malbin, D. (2002). *Trying Differently Rather Than Harder* (2nd edn). Portland, OR: FASCETS Inc.

Moradi, A.R., Doost, H.T., Taghavi, M.R., Yule, W. and Dalgeish, T. (1999). Everyday memory deficits in children and adolescents with PTSD: Performance on the Rivermead Behavioural Memory Test. *The Journal of Child Psychology and Psychiatry 40*, 3, 357–361.

Nolin, P. and Ethier, L. (2007). Using neuropsychological profiles to classify neglected children with or without physical abuse. *Child Abuse and Neglect 31*, 631–643.

Noll, J.G., Trickett, P.K., Susman, E.J. and Putnam, F.W. (2006). Sleep disturbances and childhood sexual abuse. *Journal of Pediatric Psychology 31*, 5, 469–480. doi: 10.1093/jpepsy/jsj040

Ogilvie, J., Stewart, A., Chan, R. and Shum, D. (2011). Neuropsychological measures of executive function and antisocial behaviour: A meta-analysis. *Criminology 49*, 4, 1063–1107. doi: 10.1111/j.1745-9125.2011.00252.x

Perry, B.D. (2006). Applying principles of neurodevelopment to clinical work with maltreated and traumatized children: The neurosequential model of therapeutics. In N.B. Webb (ed.) *Working with Traumatized Youth in Child Welfare: Social Work Practice with Children and Families.* New York: Guilford Press.

Perry, B.D. (2009). Examining child maltreatment through a neurodevelopmental lens: Clinical applications of the neurosequential model of therapeutics. *Journal of Loss and Trauma 14*, 240–255.

Perry, B.D. and Dobson, C.L. (2013). The neurosequential model of therapeutics. In J.D. Ford and C.A. Courtois (eds) *Treating Complex Traumatic Stress Disorders in Children and Adolescents.* New York: Guilford Press.

Pollak, S.D. and Sinha, P. (2002). Effects of early experience on children's recognition of facial displays of emotion. *Development and Psychopathology 38*, 784–791.

Pollak, S.D., Nelson, C.A., Schlaak, M.F., Roeber, B.J. *et al.* (2010). Neurodevelopmental effects of early deprivation in post-institutionalized children. *Child Development 81*, 224–236.

Prasad M.R., Kramer, L.A. and Ewing Cobbs, L. (2005). Cognitive and neuroimaging findings in physically abused preschoolers. *Archives of Disease in Childhood 90*, 82–85.

Price-Robertson, R., Higgins, D. and Vassallo, S. (2013). Multi-type maltreatment and polyvictimisation: A comparison of two research frameworks. *Family Matters 93*, 84–98. Accessed on 6/6/2018 at https://aifs.gov.au/publications/family-matters/issue-93/multi-type-maltreatment-and-polyvictimisation

Sylvestre, A., Bussières, È.L. and Bouchard, C. (2016). Language problems among abused and neglected children: A meta-analytic review. *Child Maltreatment 21*, 1, 47–58. doi: 10.1177/1077559515616703

Teicher, M.H., Anderson, C.M. and Polcari, A. (2012). Childhood maltreatment is associated with reduced volume in the hippocampal subfields CA3, dentate gyrus, and subiculum. *Proceedings of the National Academy of Sciences 109*, E563–E572.

van der Kolk, B.A., Pynoos, R.S., Cicchetti, D., Cloitre, M. *et al.* (2009). Proposal to include a developmental trauma disorder diagnosis for children and adolescents in DSM-V. Accessed on 6/6/2018 at www.traumacenter.org/announcements/DTD_papers_Oct_09.pdf

Wyper, K.R. and Rasmussen, C.R. (2011). Language impairments in children with fetal alcohol spectrum disorder. *Journal of Population Therapeutics and Clinical Pharmacology 8*, 2. e364–e376. Accessed on 6/6/2018 at www.jptcp.com/articles/language-impairments-in-children-with-fetal-alcohol-spectrum-disorders.pdf

Zilberstein, K. and Popper, S. (2014). Clinical competencies for the effective treatment of foster children. *Clinical Child Psychology and Psychiatry 21*, 1. doi: 10.1177/1359104514547597

Chapter 2

For general information about positive approaches to parenting, visit:
www.kidsmatter.edu.au/mental-health-matters/social-and-emotional-learning/managing-behaviour-making-rules
KidsMatter is an Australian website that provides a range of free information and resources on positive parenting and enhancing child wellbeing.
http://raisingchildren.net.au
The Raising Children Network provides a range of free resources and guidance on child development and positive parenting approaches.

These websites provide information about infant developmental milestones and the behaviours you would expect to see as part of normal infant development.
https://raisingchildren.net.au/newborns/development/understanding-development/baby-development
The raising children network provides a range of information about child development and parenting.
https://www.acecqa.gov.au/sites/default/files/2018-02/Developmental MilestonesEYLFandNQS.pdf
The Australian Government has produced the Early Years Learning framework which provides a guide to expected development and behaviour in an early childhood education setting; together with further links to early childhood development

Chapter 3

Department of Human Services, Victoria (2012). Child Development and Trauma: Best Interests case practice model, Specialist practice resource.

Emerson, E. (1995). *Challenging Behaviour: Analysis and Intervention in People with Learning Disabilities*. Cambridge: Cambridge University Press.

Holden, M.J. (2009). *Children and Residential Experiences: Creating Conditions for Change*. New York: Child and Family Practice.

Institute for Human Services (2007). Developmental Milestones Chart. Accessed on 3/10/2018 at www.rsd.k12.pa.us/Downloads/Development_Chart_for_Booklet.pdf

McLean, S. (2017). *Foster Parents' Guide to Child Development Milestones*. Adelaide: University of South Australia.

Ozretich, R. and Bowman, S.R. (2001). Middle childhood and adolescent development. Oregon State University. Accessed on 3/10/2018 at https://studylib.net/doc/8817322/middle-childhood-and-adolescent-development

Rycus, J.S. and Hughes, R.C. (1998). *Field Guide to Child Welfare Vol III. Child Development and Child Welfare*. Washington, DC: Child Welfare League of America Press.

Sattler, J. (2014). *Foundations of Behavioural Social and Clinical Assessment of Children* (6th edn). San Diego, CA: Pro-Ed Australia.

The following websites provide free additional information about the ages and stages in normal child development:

www.healthychildren.org/english/ages-stages/pages/default.aspx
The Healthy Children website publishes free content written by the American Academy of Pediatrics, and provides easy to understand guidance for parents on a range of issues related to child development and family wellbeing.

http://developingchild.harvard.edu/science/key-concepts
The Center on the Developing Child website was created by Harvard University and publishes free content on the latest science related to early child development.

Chapter 4

For more information about sensory processing difficulties, visit:
www.sensory-processing-disorder.com
https://sensorytools.net
www.sensorysmartparent.com/sensory-checklist.pdf
http://sensorysmarts.com/signs_of_spd.html
www.child-behavior-guide.com/sensory-processing-disorder.html
www.spdaustralia.com.au
www.sensoryprocessing.info

These websites provide more comprehensive information for non-professionals about sensory processing difficulties; and many contain additional checklists that may be useful in understanding your child's individual sensory profile and sensory preferences.

Chapter 5

Blank, M., Rose, S.A. and Berlin, L.J. (1978). *The Language of Learning: The Preschool Years*. Orlando: Grune & Stratton, Inc.

McLean, S. (2017). Foster parent's guide to language and communication difficulties. Accessed on 6/6/2018 at www.fosteringdifference.com.au/images/Resources/ForFosterParents/Fostering-Difference-Communication-and-Language.pdf

To learn more about language and communication difficulties, visit:
www.thecommunicationtrust.org.uk
The Communication Trust is a coalition of UK organisations that work together to support those who work with children with speech, language and communication difficulties. They produce a range of free resources and training that can be accessed via their website.

www.betterhealth.vic.gov.au/health/healthyliving/receptive-language-disorder
The Better Health website is an Australian government website that provides basic information about speech and language concerns and where to access support.

Chapter 6

For more information about emotional regulation strategies you can also visit the following websites.

https://childmind.org/article/can-help-kids-self-regulation

The Child Mind Institute provides parents, professionals and policy makes with a range of practical resources and information about supporting child development.

https://www.kidsmatter.edu.au/mental-health-matters/social-and-emotional-learning/emotional-development/coping-skills-managing

KidsMatter is an Australian website that provides a range of free information and resources on positive parenting and enhancing child wellbeing. The Raising Children Network provides a range of free resources and guidance on child development and positive parenting approaches.

Chapter 7

Espy, K.A. and Kaufmann, P.M. (2002). Individual differences in the development of executive function in children: Lessons from the delayed response and A-not-B tasks. In D.L. Molfese and V.J. Molfese (eds) *Developmental Variations in Learning: Applications to Social, Executive Function, Language, and Reading Skills.* Mahwah, NJ: Lawrence Erlbaum Associates.

McLean, S. (2016). The effect of trauma on the brain development of children. Evidence-based principles for supporting the recovery of children in care. CFCA Practitioner Resource, June 2016. Australian Institute of Family Studies. Accessed on 6/6/2018 at https://aifs.gov.au/cfca/publications/effect-trauma-brain-development-children

McLean, S. and McDougall, S. (2014). Fetal alcohol spectrum disorders: Current issues in awareness, prevention and intervention. CFCA Paper 29. Melbourne: Australian Institute for Family Studies.

Martel, M., Pan, P., Hoffman, M., Gadelha, A., do Rosario, M.C, Mari, J.J. *et al.* (2017). A general psychopathology factor (P factor) in children: Structural model analysis and external validation through familial risk and child global executive function. *Journal of Abnormal Psychology* 126, 1, 137–148.

Morgan, A.B. and Lilienfeld, S.O. (2000). A meta-analytic review of the relation between antisocial behavior and neuropsychological measures of executive function. *Clinical Psychology Review 20*, 113–136.

For more information about executive functioning difficulties, visit:

www.understood.org/en/learning-attention-issues/child-learning-disabilities/executive-functioning-issues/executive-functioning-issues-strategies-you-can-try-at-home

Understood is an American website dedicated to supporting parents raising children with learning and attention difficulties. It offers free resources, an online support community and expert advice.

Chapter 8

American Psychiatric Association (2013). *Diagnostic and Statistical Manual of Mental Disorders* (5th edn). Arlington, VA: American Psychiatric Publishing.

Anda, R.F., Felitti, V.J. and Bremner, J.D. (2006). The enduring effects of abuse and related adverse experiences in childhood: A convergence of evidence from neurobiology and epidemiology. *European Archives of Psychiatry and Clinical Neuroscience 256*, 174–186.

Bakker, D., Kazantzis, N., Rickwood, D. and Rickard, N. (2016). Mental health smartphone apps: Review and evidence-based recommendations for future developments. *JMIR Mental Health 3*, 1, e7. Accessed on 6/6/2018 at http://doi.org/10.2196/mental.4984

Beidas, P., Stewart, R., Walsh, L., Lucas, S. *et al.* (2015). Free, brief, and validated: Standardized instruments for low resource mental health settings. *Cognitive Behavioral Practice 22*, 1, 5–19. doi:10.1016/j.cbpra.2014.02.002

Berridge, K.C., Robinson, T.E. and Aldreige, J.W. (2009). Dissecting components of reward: 'Liking', 'wanting' and learning. *Current Opinion in Pharmacology 9*, 65–73.

Bubier, J.L. and Drabick, D.A.G. (2009). Co-occurring anxiety and disruptive behavior disorders: The roles of anxious symptoms, reactive aggression, and shared risk processes. *Clinical Psychology Review 29*, 7, 658–669. doi:10.1016/j.cpr.2009.08.005

Donker, T., Griffiths, K., Cuijpers, P. and Christensen, H. (2009). Psycho-education for depression, anxiety and psychological distress. *BMC Medicine 7*, 7–79. doi: 10.1186/1741-7015-7-79

Ford, T., Vostanis, P., Meltzer, H. and Goodman, R. (2007). Psychiatric disorder among British children looked after by local authorities: Comparison with children living in private households. *British Journal of Psychiatry 190*, 319–325. doi: 10.1192/bjp.bp.106.025023

Froh, J.J., Bono, G., Fan, J., Emmons, R.A. *et al.* (2014). Nice thinking. An educational intervention that teaches children to think gratefully. *School Psychology Review 43*, 2, 132–152.

Green, J.G., McLaughlin, K.A., Berglund, P.A., Gruber, M.J. *et al.* (2010). Childhood adversities and adult psychiatric disorders in the national comorbidity survey replication I: Associations with first onset of DSM-IV disorders. *Archives of General Psychiatry 67*, 113–123.

Kangas, M. (2014). Treatment guidance for common mental health disorders: Anxiety. *InPsych 36*, 5. Accessed on 3/10/2018 at https://www.psychology.org.au/inpsych/2014/october/kangas

Kinniburgh, K., Blaustein, M., Spinazzola, J. and van der Kolk, B. (2005). Attachment, self-regulation and competency. *Psychiatric Annals 35*, 5, 424–430.

Luke, N., Sinclair, I., Woolgar, M. and Sebba, J. (2014). What works in preventing and treating poor mental health in looked after children? NSPCC and Oxford University. Accessed on 6/6/2018 at www.nspcc.org.uk/globalassets/documents/evaluation-of-services/preventing-treating-mental-health-looked-after-children-summary

McCrory, E., De Brito, S.A. and Viding, E. (2010). Research review: The neurobiology and genetics of maltreatment and adversity. *The Journal of Child Psychology and Psychiatry 51*, 1079–1095.

McCrory, E., Gerin, M.L. and Viding, E. (2017). Annual Research Review: Childhood maltreatment, latent vulnerability and the shift to preventative psychiatry – the contribution of functional brain imaging. *The Journal of Child Psychology and Psychiatry 58*, 4, 338–357.

McLean, S. (2016). The effect of trauma on the brain development of children. Evidence-based principles for supporting the recovery of children in care. CFCA Practitioner Resource, June 2016. Australian Institute of Family Studies. Accessed on 6/6/2018 at https://aifs.gov.au/cfca/publications/effect-trauma-brain-development-children

McLean, S. (2018a). Developmental differences in children who have experienced adversity: Diminished social reward (practice guide 2 of 4). CFCA Practitioner Resource, May 2018. Australian Institute of Family Studies. Accessed on 3/10/2018 at https://aifs.gov.au/cfca/publications/developmental-differences/diminished-social-reward

McLean, S. (2018b). Developmental differences in children who have experienced adversity: Threat bias (practice guide 4 of 4). CFCA Practitioner Resource, May 2018. Australian Institute of Family Studies. Accessed on 3/10/2018 at https://aifs.gov.au/cfca/publications/developmental-differences/threat-bias

Muris, P. and Field, A. (2008). Distorted cognition and pathological anxiety in children and adolescents. *Cognition and Emotion 22*, 3, 395–421. https://doi.org/10.1080/02699930701843450

Öhman, A. (2009). Of snakes and faces: An evolutionary perspective on the psychology of fear. *Scandinavian Journal of Psychology 50*, 543–552.

Öhman, A., Carlsson, K., Lundqvist, D. and Ingvar, M. (2007). On the unconscious subcortical origin of human fear. *Physiology & Behavior 92*, 180–185.

Pineau, H., Marchand, A. and Guay, S. (2014). Objective neuropsychological deficits in post-traumatic stress disorder and mild traumatic brain injury: What remains beyond symptom similarity? *Behavioural Sciences 4*, 471–486. doi:10.3390/bs4040471

Price-Robertson, R., Higgins, D. and Vassallo, S. (2013). Multi-type maltreatment and polyvictimisation: A comparison of two research frameworks. *Family Matters 93*, 84–98. Accessed on 6/6/2018 at https://aifs.gov.au/publications/family-matters/issue-93/multi-typemaltreatment-and-polyvictimisation

Reinecke, L., Dattilio, F. and Freeman, A. (2003). *Cognitive Therapy with Children and Adolescents: A Casebook for Clinical Practice.* New York: Guilford Press.

Seligman, M., Ernst, R.M., Gillam, J., Reivich, K. and Linkins, M. (2009). Positive education: Positive psychology and classroom interventions. *Oxford Review of Education 35*, 293–311.

Sinha, R. (2008). Chronic stress, drug use, and vulnerability to addiction. *Annals of the New York Academy of Sciences 1141*, 105–130. http://doi.org/10.1196/annals.1441.030

Vachon, D.D., Krueger, R.F., Rogosch, F.A. and Cicchetti, D. (2015). Assessment of the harmful psychiatric and behavioral effects of different forms of maltreatment. *JAMA Psychiatry 72*, 1135–1142.

Weare, K. and Hind, M. (2011). Mental health promotion and problem prevention in schools: What does the evidence say? *Health Promotion International 26*, i29–i69.

Winsor, T. and McLean, S. (2016). Residential group care workers' recognition of depression: Assessment of mental health literacy using clinical vignettes. *Children and Youth Services Review 68*, 132–138. https://doi.org/10.1016/j.childyouth.2016.06.028

YoungMinds (n.d.). Beyond Adversity: Addressing the mental health needs of young people who face complexity and adversity in their lives. Accessed on 3/10/2018 at https://youngminds.org.uk/media/1241/report_-_beyond_adversity.pdf

For more resources and worksheets on developing resilience in vulnerable children, see the following websites:

https://childmind.org/article/behavioral-treatment-kids-anxiety
The Child Mind Institute is an organisation dedicated to supporting children and families struggling with mental health and learning disorders.

http://childrenwithanxiety.com
The Children's Anxiety Institute aims to support children and families living with anxiety. It provides resources developed by parents, for parents supporting anxious children.

https://www.innerhealthstudio.com/relaxation-scripts-for-children.html
Inner Health Studio provides a mix of relaxation scripts and audio for purchase, and some free resources.

http://raisingchildren.net.au/articles/anxiety_stepladder_approach.html
The Raising Children Network provides a range of free resources and guidance on child development and positive parenting approaches.

For more information about communicating assertively, see

https://positivepsychologyprogram.com/assertiveness/
Positive Psychology provides a range of free introductory resources about positive psychology and assertive communication.

Appendix A

MY SENSORY 'LIKES' THESE THINGS HELP ME STAY CALM	
SIGHT	
TOUCH	
HEARING	
SMELL	
TASTE	

Appendix B

MY SENSORY 'DISLIKES' THESE THINGS STRESS ME OUT	
SIGHT	
TOUCH	
HEARING	
SMELL	
TASTE	

Appendix C

MY SENSORY PLAN	
THESE THINGS HELP ME STAY FOCUSED	
	SIGHT
	TOUCH
	HEARING
	SMELL
	TASTE
	MOVING MY BODY
	USING BIG MUSCLES

Subject Index

Author Index